LION BRAND YARN

JUST**BAGS**

Also by Lion Brand Yarn

Lion Brand Yarn: Just Hats

Lion Brand Yarn: Just Scarves

Lion Brand Yarn: Vintage Styles for Today

LION BRAND YARN

JUST BAGS

30 PATTERNS TO KNIT AND CROCHET

EDITED BY STEPHANIE KLOSE AND CATHY MAGUIRE

NEW YORK

The authors and publisher would like to thank the Craft Yarn Council of America for providing the yarn weight standards and accompanying icons used in this book. For more information, please visit www.YarnStandards.com.

Published in the United States by
Potter Craft, an imprint of the
Crown Publishing Group, a division of
Random House, Inc., New York.

POTTER CRAFT and CLARKSON N. POTTER are trademarks and POTTER and colophon are registered trademarks of Random House, Inc.

Printed in Singapore

Design by Caitlin Daniels Israel
Editors: Stephanie Klose and Cathy Maguire
Photography: Jack Deutsch

Library of Congress Cataloging-in-Publication

ISBN: 0-307-20993-8

10 9 8 7 6 5 4 3 2 1

First Edition

CONTENTS

INTRODUCTION

Whether you prefer glamorous, frivolous designer bags or a practical, sturdy, everyday carryall, bags are a crucial part of modern attire. Make your own one-of-a-kind bag with all the hallmarks of the haute couture accessory, or personalize your bag to suit your busy life.

Just Bags celebrates the bag and presents both knit and crochet patterns for a wide variety of styles. Easy-to-follow knit and crochet instructions are accompanied by directions for specialized construction methods like linings and reinforcements. Particular attention is paid to useful accessories and hardware that promise both practicality and panache. Multicolored yarns that range from fine to super bulky are knit, crocheted, woven, and felted to produce an array of new and interesting textures. A whole host of color and yarn textures range from soft yarns to glitzy yarns as well as classic staples.

Each of the seven chapters in this book gradually introduces new skills and tips that clarify the many steps that go into the construction of a successful bag. Beginners will want to start with the simple patterns in chapter 1 and work their way up to the later chapters that cover more specialized knitting and crocheting techniques, including granny squares (chapters 1 and 2), patchwork knitting (chapter 3), weave crocheting (chapter 5), and double-hem finishing (chapter 5). Specific construction techniques such as lining (chapters 3, 4, and 7), hardware (chapters 2 and 5) and felting (chapter 6) can be learned and adapted for future projects.

We assume you know the basic knitting skills of knit and purl, and the basic crochet skills of single crochet, double crochet, and half double crochet. If you need to learn the basic stitches or refresh your memory, there are a number of free resources. Learntoknit.com, learntocrochet.com, and lionbrand.com offer good introductions for first-timers. Crochet.about.com and knitting.about.com provide tutorials on more advanced techniques and forums for asking questions of on-staff experts. Your local library can be a valuable resource for basic knitting and crochet reference books.

There's also a wealth of knowledge to be gained from experienced knitters and crocheters. Most knitting and crochet guilds welcome new members, and many yarn and craft shops offer group classes in knit and crochet. Ask around for local groups who organize "knit and network" meetings at coffee shops, and listen for "knit and bitch" groups you can join. You might be surprised by the number of knitters and crocheters you'll run into. From commuters who stitch away the hours on subways and buses across the country to Hollywood starlets and ex-con business tycoons, stitchers are everywhere; you only have to seek to find a few friends familiar with needles and hooks.

This book follows the standards and guidelines created by the Craft Yarn Council of America to help you choose patterns that are right for your skill level. Each pattern is labeled as Beginner, Easy, Intermediate, or Experienced. Beginner patterns are suitable for first-time knitters and crocheters and only require basic stitch skills. Easy patterns call for basic stitches, repetitive pattern work, simple color changes, simple shaping, and finishing. Intermediate patterns include a variety of stitches and techniques, such as lacework, simple intarsia, double-pointed needles, and finishing. Projects using complicated techniques, such as short rows, multicolor changes, complicated cables, lace patterns, detailed shaping, finishing, and using fine threads are for experienced knitters and crocheters.

CHOOSING YOUR YARN

Bags can be made with just about any yarn, but special consideration should be given to the function and durability of your design. If you want a sturdy, self-supporting bag, then choose a denser yarn like cotton or worsted-weight wool. If you have your heart set on a soft yarn, simply blend it with a stronger yarn or make the bag with a reinforced lining. Strengthen your bag with a firmer gauge than you would use for a wearable

STANDARD YARN WEIGHT SYSTEM

YARN WEIGHT SYMBOL & CATEGORY NAMES	1 SUPER FINE	2 FINE	3 LIGHT	4 MEDIUM	5 BULKY	6 SUPER BULKY
TYPE OF YARNS IN CATEGORY	Sock, Fingering, Baby	Sport, Baby	DK, Light Worsted	Worsted, Afghan, Aran	Chunky, Craft, Rug	Bulky, Roving
KNIT GAUGE RANGE* IN STOCKINETTE STITCH TO 4 INCHES	27–32 sts	23–26 sts	21–24 sts	16–20 sts	12–15 sts	6–11 sts
RECOMMENDED NEEDLE IN METRIC SIZE RANGE	2.25–3.25 mm	3.25–3.75 mm	3.75–4.5 mm	4.5–5.5 mm	5.5–8 mm	8 mm and larger
RECOMMENDED NEEDLE U.S. SIZE RANGE	1 to 3	3 to 5	5 to 7	7 to 9	9 to 11	11 and larger
CROCHET GAUGE* RANGES IN SINGLE CROCHET TO 4 INCH	21–32 sts	16–20 sts	12–17 sts	11–14 sts	8–11 sts	5–9 sts
RECOMMENDED HOOK IN METRIC SIZE RANGE	2.25–3.5 mm	3.5–4.5 mm	4.5–5.5 mm	5.5–6.5 mm	6.5–9 mm	9 mm and larger
RECOMMENDED HOOK U.S. SIZE RANGE	B–1 to E–4	E–4 to 7	7 to I–9	I–9 to K–10½	K–10½ to M–13	M–13 and larger

***Guidelines only:** The above reflect the most commonly used gauges and needle or hook sizes for specific yarn categories.

project. Soft, stretchy bags like vintage mesh "grocery bags" are still great to knit or crochet, but they have limitations.

Yarn choices depend on the end use of your bag. Wool, wool blends, acrylics, and chenilles work wonderfully for reliable fall/winter day bags and totes. Cotton, cotton blends, microfiber yarns, and ribbon yarns are more suitable for spring/summer bags. Fur and metallic yarns are excellent for glamorous, year-round evening bags.

In today's marketplace there is a dazzling array of yarns. Knowing the inherent qualities of each type of yarn will give you the best results when you experiment with different texture combinations. Traditional smooth yarns give good stitch definition and are great for trying different stitch patterns or experimenting with color. In a variety of gauges from super fine to extra bulky, these yarns come in a wide range of fibers and blends to fit any project or budget.

Brushed yarns produce a "halo" of hairlike fiber and work well on large needles and hooks in simple stitches. They include mohair, mohair blends, angora, and synthetic yarns that imitate the brushed look. Chenille yarn looks and feels like velvet. It is best to knit and crochet this yarn at a firm gauge.

Other yarns are heavily textured. Bouclés, for instance, are a "loopy" yarn, which can help to hide a multitude of stitching sins. They are best used on larger needles and hooks. They work up fast and are as fun to make as they are to wear. One caution: Make sure to pick up the entire thread and not to catch your needle or hook on the "loop" part on the yarn only. Eyelash yarns make great accents or can be used for complete projects when mixed with other yarns. Since the "lash" part of the yarn is often connected by a thin thread, eyelash yarns can easily be worked with other yarns to produce subtly sensational effects. Try combining two different colors of eyelash to create a mélange of colors.

A good rule of thumb with any fancy or textured yarn is "less is more." Save the fancy stitch work for smoother yarns. Let the dazzling yarn do the work for you.

SUBSTITUTING YARN

All the projects featured in this book were made with Lion Brand yarn. If you want to duplicate the item shown exactly, simply head to your local craft shop or online retailer and purchase the yarn noted in the pattern information. If you want to substitute a different yarn, simply purchase a yarn with a similar weight and fiber content, as noted in the pattern information.

When describing yarn, terms like "bulky" or "sport weight" can mean different things to different people. The Craft Yarn Council of America has established guidelines called the Standard Yarn Weight System to standardize descriptions of yarn thickness. The materials section of each pattern in this book features an icon of a skein of yarn with a number on it. That number corresponds to one of these categories. The guiding principle of this system is the smaller the number, the thinner the yarn.

NEEDLES/HOOKS

As you become more experienced as a knitter or crocheter, you will develop a preference for a certain type of needle or hook. Needles and hooks range from plastic and metal to bamboo and exotic woods like ebony—some are even gold plated! Beginner crocheters might want to consider buying hooks that have soft molded heads and avoid carved hooks with sharp-cut heads. Use whatever makes you most comfortable. Sometimes it is beneficial to knit back and forth on circular needles (instead of on straight needles) because the cord connecting the needles can accommodate more stitches. Circular needles also make large, heavy projects a little easier to control and handle.

OTHER TOOLS

Scissors and a tape measure are a must. Often sizes are not imprinted on circular needles made from bamboo, wood, or metal, so a good needle gauge (with inches and centimeters) is recommended. It's handy to have a large-eyed, blunt needle for finishing and weaving in ends. You might find it useful to have stitch markers and cable needles for certain projects as well.

FINDING YOUR GAUGE

Getting your gauge may be a new concept if you haven't been knitting or crocheting for long. In general, gauge (sometimes called tension) is the number of stitches and rows measured over a number of inches (or centimeters) of your fabric. Every knitter or crocheter has her or his own particular tension, even when using the same needles and yarn as another person, so it is important to make sure you get the accurate gauge in order to make a bag that will be the correct size indicated in the pattern.

You need to knit or crochet a swatch to find your gauge number, or "G" number. As a starting place, use the needle or hook size recommended by the manufacturer on the yarn label. Needles and hooks are sized in two ways: the actual size measured in millimeters (mm) and a descriptive size. Knitting needles have descriptive sizes that are expressed in numbers and crochet hooks have descriptive sizes that are expressed in letters. For example, 5 mm knitting needles are size 8, and 5 mm crochet hooks are size H-8.

Knit or crochet a swatch in the stitch called for by your project that is *at least* 4" (10 cm) wide. With a ruler, count the number of stitches in a 4" (10 cm) width (including half-stitches if there are any). Divide this number by 4 and you have your "G" number, or *the number of stitches per inch*. It is a good idea to take this measurement at a few different places on the fabric and average them. Your number may have half- or quarter-stitches represented as a decimal point if you did your division on a calculator.

If you did not get very close to the gauge in the pattern, switch needles and try again: go up a needle size if your gauge is too tight, or down a needle size if your gauge is too loose.

Many people knit and crochet for years before they ever do a knit or crochet gauge swatch. Once you start, you'll never do another project without one. Most swatches can be made in less than thirty minutes and it's worth taking the time. There's no need to keep your gauge swatch as long as you save the right information. Photocopy the swatch and make sure you save the yarn details (brand name and standardized weight), needle or hook size, stitch pattern (e.g., stockinette or single crochet), number of stitches, number of rows, and the corresponding "G" number. It's good to start a file or a binder keeping your gauge information. You can avoid having to redo a gauge swatch for a new project made from a yarn you are already familiar with. Your gauge information can be saved by standardized weight or by yarn company. Familiarizing yourself with different gauges may encourage you to experiment with sizing and developing your own designs.

SIZING

The patterns for the bags in this book are written in one size only. There's nothing to stop you from scaling the bag down or up. All you need is a gauge swatch to work it out. If this is your first time adapting a pattern, choose a design from chapter 1 and work your way up to a more complicated pattern. For example, the Easiest Knit Bag Ever on page 17 has instructions for knitting an 8" wide by 9" long (20.5 x 23 cm) bag. The bag is knit in one piece and folded in half so the panel is knit 8" wide by 18" long (20.4 x 45.5 cm). The gauge is: 8 stitches and 16 rows = 4" (10 cm), and the "G" number is 2 stitches and 4 rows.

To make the same bag in a bigger size use the "G" number and adjust the pattern. For a finished bag 10" wide by 12" long (25.5 x 30.5 cm), double the length. This bag will be knit in one piece and folded in half so that the panel is knit 10" wide by 24" long (25.5 x 61 cm). Simply multiply the "G" number of stitches by 10 (for the width) and the "G" number of rows by 24 (for the length): 20 stitches and 96 rows. Follow the instructions with the new number of stitches and rows.

MAKING YOUR BAG STURDY

LININGS

A well-built lining will make your bag durable and sturdy while protecting the yarn and seams from snagging or wearing on the inside. Lining a bag offers an interesting alternative to knit or crocheted patterns that aren't reversible, and at the same time enhances the overall design of your bag. Linings can be machine- or hand-stitched, half-lined or fully lined; they can even be constructed without any sewing.

Linings can maintain the shape of your bag and provide stability, especially when working with soft or stretchy yarns. The knitted and crocheted evening bags in chapter 4, with Fun Fur and Fancy Fur accents, have full linings made from felt and ultrasuede, respectively. Both linings extend beyond the inside of the bag to form the opening placket. Without the lining, the shell shape would collapse under the weight of the yarn. The linings also act as a barrier to prevent the Fun Fur and Fancy Fur from catching on the inside.

The reinforced felt lining used for the crocheted Venus Clutch in chapter 4 is put together in a few easy steps. Commercial felt (or ultrasuede) won't fray, so there is no need to finish the seams. The knitted Log Cabin Tote in chapter 3 is a great example of a no-sew lining. The fusible adhesive that attaches the lining to the knitted panels also acts as a stabilizer and stiffener to stop the yarn from stretching.

In chapter 7, the Felt Trim Tote is a good example of a partially lined bag. It has a reinforced muslin lining on a three-sided border. The front and back remain unlined. The base of the Knit and Go Tote in chapter 5 has a reinforced self lining. Two bases are knit and stitched together with plastic canvas encased in between.

All the lining techniques in this book can be easily adapted to accommodate most knit or crochet designs.

INTERFACING

Interfacing your bag is a practical choice and there are many fun and creative ways to do it. Most of the reinforcement materials used for this book were designed for other crafts (needlepoint) or purposes (gardening).

One of the most practical products on the market is plastic canvas mesh. It is a plastic mesh sold in 13.5" by 11" (34.5 x 28 cm) sheets, 4" (10 cm) circles, as well as all kinds of novelty shapes (stars and hearts). It is manufactured in several gauges to match different weight yarns. Plastic canvas was originally designed for three-dimensional needlepoint and is sold in many different colors. Many of the patterns in the book use plastic canvas as an additional support for linings, borders, and bag openings. The plastic is sturdy and the holes in the grid make it easy to sew. It can also be used more traditionally and wrapped (or covered) in the same yarn, such as the ends of the Yoga Bag in chapter 5.

Several unconventional supplies were used to reinforce handles. Standard airline tubing and Orbit Drip Master soaker tubing can be found at a good hardware store. They can be covered in purchased fabric, with a knit or crochet tube, or they can simply be wrapped and covered with yarn. Both products are pliable and can be put through the hot wash cycles for felted bags.

See Get a Handle On It in chapter 2 for a quirky approach to a sturdy bag handle. The handles are made from container lids.

Nylon webbing has been used in three designs for straps and handles that extend all the way around the bag. The nylon webbing keeps the bag from stretching and gives the designs that "urban chic" finish.

GREAT HARDWARE

The right hardware can change the look of a basic knit or crochet bag into a finished, sophisticated design. If you want to contrast or complement the knit or crochet body of your bag with purchased hardware, there are many options. Handles come in hundreds of styles and all kinds of materials. Web sites like mjtrim.com and umx.info/purse-handbag-cat1.htm sell handbag handles made from a variety of materials and in a vast range of styles, shapes, and sizes. Handles can also be purchased from craft stores, such as Michael's and JoAnn's. For a unique, vintage look, buy bags at thrift shops and reuse the handles and other hardware.

Other purse-making supplies such as buckles, D-rings, magnet snap closures, swivel clasps, and tab closures are featured in designs in this book. Closures such as the magnet snap used in the All About Evening bags on pages 60–63 and the plastic center release buckle used for the Yoga Bag on page 68 are as much a design feature as they are safety and security measures.

FUN FINISHES

Even the simplest bag becomes a stunning success when you use a great finishing technique. Finish your bag with a reinforcing stitching technique or jazz up your bag with self trims like pom-poms, tassels, rope cords, and webbing.

STITCHES

These stitches can be done in the same yarn as your project or in a contrasting yarn or thread. When using any of these stitches on a purchased fabric such as felt or ultrasuede use a cotton embroidery floss instead of yarn.

Running Stitch (used to top stitch)

This basic sewing stitch looks fresh and new when done with yarn on knitted or crocheted fabric. Use a running stitch to topstitch webbing, handles, and bag closures. Use a blunt, large-eyed needle and insert it into the fabric from the wrong side to the right side, leaving a 3" (7.5 cm) tail of yarn to weave in later. Insert the needle back to the wrong side and be careful not to pull the yarn too tightly or it will distort the fabric. Continue for desired length and fasten off on wrong side of piece.

Blanket Stitch

Sometimes called buttonhole stitch, blanket stitch is a great finishing touch on edges (see page 60). Blanket stitch has been used to finish handles and bag edges, but can also be used to embellish.

Step 1. Using a blunt, large-eyed yarn needle, secure the yarn by gently attaching it to a stitch on the wrong side of work. Leave a 3" (8 cm) tail to weave in later.

Step 2. Draw the needle through to the right side of work, close to the edge.

Step 3. Bring the needle above the yarn and insert it a couple of stitches to the right of where you first inserted it (see illustration A).

Step 4. Pull the needle past the edge of the bag to complete the stitch.

Repeat Steps 3 and 4, inserting the needle the same number of stitches apart for even spacing.

Invisible Seaming

Invisible seaming is a sturdy, invisible way to sew two panels together. It can be sewn (vertically) on the side seam or (horizontally) on two-bound off edges. Invisible seaming is worked on the right side, with a long yarn end (add a length from the initial cast-on or bound-off edge) and a blunt, large-eyed

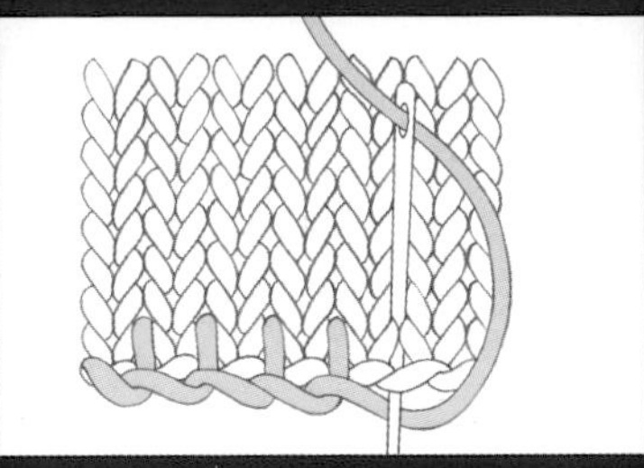
A. Blanket stitch.

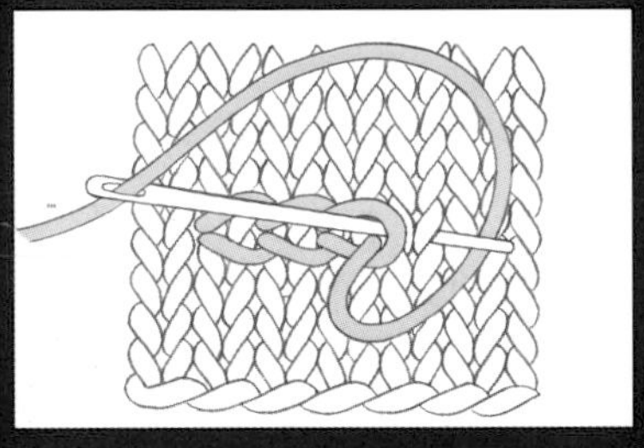
B. Chain stitch.

C. Invisible seam—stockinette stitch.

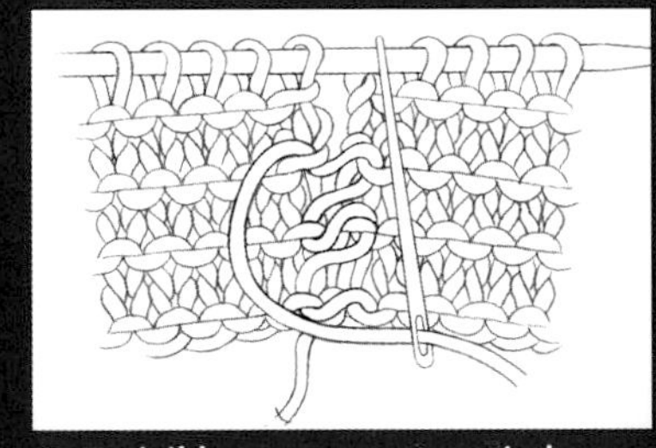
D. Invisible seam—garter stitch.

sewing needle. Start at the upper or lower edge by joining the two edges. Begin the seaming by catching two horizontal bars just inside the edge of the first stitch and carry the thread across to the other side, stitching under the next pair of bars inside the edge of the first stitch (see illustration B). Pull the sewing thread every couple of stitches but do not gather. There should be some ease. The seam will join together and be nearly invisible. The same technique can be used to join two bound-off edges see illustration C).

TRIMS AND EMBELLISHMENTS

Fun and funky embellishments on projects in this book include an evening bag with feather trim, an all-white granny square bag with cowry shells sewn in the centers, an Easter bag with polymer clay carrots, and a bag with crocheted grapes. Knit and crochet flowers make a versatile embellishment for any bag.

Rope Cords

Cut six strands of yarn, each approximately 94" (239 cm) long. (If you are using a bulky yarn for the tie, you may want to use fewer than six strands of yarn to make the cord.) Hold the lengths together and tie a knot at each end. Anchor one end and twist the other end clockwise many times until the piece is very tight and almost kinked. Hold the rope in the center and release both ends, allowing them to wrap around each other.

Crochet Flowers

Chain 4. Join with slip stitch to form a ring.

Round 1 Chain 1 (counts as 1 single crochet), work 11 single crochet into ring. Join round with slip stitch in chain-1.

Round 2 (Chain 3, skip next stitch, single crochet in next stitch) 6 times—6 chain-3 loops.

Round 3 (In next chain-3 loop work [single crochet, half double crochet, 3 double crochet, half double crochet, single crochet]) 6 times. Join round with a slip stitch in first single crochet. Fasten off.

Knit Flowers

Cast on 42 stitches.

Row 1 (wrong side) Purl.

Row 2 Knit 2, *knit 1, slip this stitch back to left needle, lift next 5 stitches on left needle over this stitch and off needle, yarn over twice, knit the first stitch again, knit 2; repeat from *—27 stitches.

Row 3 Purl 1, *purl 2 together, drop 1 of the yarn over loops, (knit into the front and back) twice in remaining yarn over of previous row, purl 1; repeat from * to last stitch, purl 1–32 stitches.

Row 4 Knit 1, *knit 3 together; repeat from *, end knit 1–12 stitches.

Row 5 *Purl 2 together; repeat from *–6 stitches; slip 2nd, 3rd, 4th, 5th, and 6th stitches over first stitch. Fasten off and sew seam.

Make another if desired. Use contrasting color to attach to bag.

1.

EASY DOES IT

The three bags in this chapter are as basic as they come, so they're perfect for beginners. The furry yarns steal the show. The self-handled Easiest Knit and Crochet Bags Ever are basic rectangles, folded in half and sewn up the sides. The Night on the Town Bag kicks the simple bag up a notch, and is the perfect first evening bag project.

THE EASIEST KNIT BAG EVER

DESIGNED BY STEPHANIE KLOSE

KNIT/BEGINNER

A perfect first project for a beginning knitter. The design is simple, and the chunky yarn makes for quick knitting—and almost instant gratification!

SIZE

8" wide x 9" long (20.5 x 23 cm), excluding Handle

MATERIALS

LION BRAND FUN FUR STRIPES
100% POLYESTER 1½ OZ (40 G)
57 YD (52 M) BALL

1 ball #300 Cotton Candy (A) or color of your choice

LION BRAND HOMESPUN
98% ACRYLIC, 2% POLYESTER
6 OZ (170 G) 185 YD (167 M) SKEIN

1 skein #385 Fuchsia (B) or color of your choice

- Size 13 (9 mm) knitting needles *or size to obtain gauge*
- Large-eyed, blunt needle

GAUGE

8 stitches + 16 rows = 4" (10 cm) in garter stitch (knit every row) with 1 strand each of A and B held together.
Be sure to check your gauge.

BAG

With 1 strand each of A and B held together, cast on 16 stitches. Work in garter stitch until piece measures 18" (45.5 cm) from beginning. Bind off.

HANDLE

Cast on 60 stitches. Bind off.

FINISHING

Fold Bag in half and sew side seams. Attach handle to Bag at side seams. Weave in ends.

THE EASIEST CROCHET BAG EVER

DESIGNED BY NICOLE TORRES

CROCHET/BEGINNER

Basic stitches and chunky yarns make quick work of this beginner crochet bag.

SIZE

7" wide x 9" long [18 x 23 cm), excluding Handle

MATERIALS

LION BRAND HOMESPUN
98% ACRYLIC, 2% POLYESTER
6 OZ (170 G) 185 YD (167 M)
SKEIN

1 skein #365 Corinthian (A) or color of your choice

LION BRAND FUN FUR
100% POLYESTER 1¾ OZ (50 G)
64 YD (58 M) BALL

2 balls #191 Violet (B) or color of your choice

- Size N-13 (9 mm) crochet hook *or size to obtain gauge*
- Large-eyed, blunt needle

GAUGE

8.5 single crochet = 4" (10 cm) with 1 strand each of A and B held together.

Be sure to check your gauge.

BAG

With 1 strand each of A and B together, chain 16.

Row 1 Single crochet in 2nd chain from hook and in each chain across. Turn—15 stitches.

Row 2 Chain 1, single crochet in each single crochet across. Turn.

Repeat Row 2 until piece measures 18" (45.5 cm). Fasten off.

Fold Bag in half and sew side seams. Weave in ends.

HANDLE

Chain 64. Single crochet in 2nd chain from hook and in each chain across. Fasten off. Sew to Bag at side seams.

NIGHT ON THE TOWN BAG

DESIGNED BY STEPHANIE KLOSE

KNIT/EASY

This bag is just a square with eyelets around the edges. Weave a drawstring through the holes and gather it into a handle.

SIZE

11" (28 cm) square before gathering to close, excluding Drawstring

MATERIALS

LION BRAND GLITTERSPUN
60% ACRYLIC, 13% POLYESTER, 27% CUPRO 1¾ OZ (50 G) 115 YD (105 M) BALL

1 ball #150 Silver (MC) or color of your choice

LION BRAND FESTIVE FUR
80% POLYESTER 20% METALLIC POLYESTER 1¾ OZS (50 G) 55 YD (50 M) BALL

1 ball #150 Silver (CC) or color of your choice

- Size 13 (9 mm) knitting needles *or size to obtain gauge*
- Size H-8 (5 mm) crochet hook

GAUGE

11 stitches + 22 rows = 4" (10 cm) in garter stitch (knit every row) with 1 strand each of MC and CC held together.
Be sure to check your gauge.

STITCH EXPLANATION

k2tog Knit two stitches together (right-slanting decrease).

BAG

With 1 strand each of MC and CC held together, cast on 30 stitches.
Knit 2 rows.
Row 1 Knit 2, (yarn over, k2tog, knit 1) 9 times, knit 1.
Rows 2–4 Knit.
Row 5 Knit 2, yarn over, k2tog, knit until 3 stitches remain, yarn over, k2tog, knit 1.
Repeat Rows 2–5 for 12 more times.
Knit 3 rows.
Repeat Row 1.
Knit 1 row.
Bind off loosely. Weave in ends.

DRAWSTRING

With MC, chain 90. Slip stitch in each chain across. Fasten off. Weave in ends.

ASSEMBLY

Beginning at any corner of Bag, thread drawstring through yarn over holes across all 4 edges of square. Pull ends to close.

2.

GET A HOLD OF THESE HANDLES

Liven up your knit and crochet bags with distinctive handles. Purchased handles will make your bag sturdier and provide a quirky contrast to the knit or crocheted fabric. The handles in this chapter will give you a good idea of different styles and how best to use them. Get a Handle On It uses container lids covered with a round of crochet for handles. The patterns cover new topics, like granny squares, along with knitting and crocheting stripes.

CRÈME DE LA CRÈME

DESIGNED BY PATTY WENIGER

CROCHET/INTERMEDIATE

This chic, tone-on-tone granny square bag uses a classic bamboo handle to accentuate its summery appeal.

SIZE

13" wide x 13" tall (33 x 33 cm)

MATERIALS

LION BRAND LION COTTON
100% COTTON SOLIDS 5 OZ (140 G) 236 YD (212 M) BALL
PRINTS 4 OZ (112 G) 189 YD (170 M) BALL

1 ball #098 Natural (A) or color of your choice

LION BRAND WOOL-EASE
80% ACRYLIC, 20% WOOL
3 OZ (85 G) 197 YD (180 M) BALL

1 ball #099 Fisherman (B) or color of your choice

LION BRAND FUN FUR
100% POLYESTER 1¾ OZ (50 G)
64 YD (58.5 M) BALL

2 balls #124 Champagne (C) or color of your choice

- Size K-10.5 (6.5 mm) crochet hook *or size to obtain gauge*
- 1 set of 15½" long (39.5 cm) bamboo purse handles
- Six ¾" (19 mm) drilled cowrie shells or shell beads (optional)
- Sewing needle and matching thread

GAUGE

Round 1 of Square 1 = 1¾" (4.5 cm) across.
Each Square = 4¼" x 4¼" (11 x 11 cm).
Be sure to check your gauge.

SQUARE 1—MAKE 4

With B, chain 4. Join with slip stitch to form ring.

Round 1 (Right Side) Chain 3, 2 double crochet in ring, chain 2, (3 double crochet, chain 2) 3 times in ring. Join with slip stitch in top of beginning chain. Turn—4 corner chain 2-spaces.

Round 2 (Wrong Side) Slip stitch in first chain 2-space, chain 3, 2 double crochet in chain 2-space, chain 1, (3 double crochet, chain 1, 3 double crochet, chain 1) in each chain 2-space around, ending with 3 double crochet in first chain 2-space already holding 2 double crochet, chain 1. Join with slip stitch in top of beginning chain. Turn—4 corner chain 1-spaces; 1 chain 1-space on each side.

Round 3 (Right Side) Slip stitch in first corner chain 1-space, chain 3, 2 double crochet in same chain 1-space, *skip next 3 double crochet, double crochet in next chain 1-space, working in front of previous round, double crochet in next corresponding double crochet 2 rounds below, double crochet in same chain 1-space in current round, skip next 3 double crochet, [3 double crochet, chain 1, 3 double crochet] in next corner chain 1-space; repeat from * around, ending with 3 double crochet in

first chain 1-space already holding 2 double crochet, chain 1. Join with slip stitch in top of beginning chain.

Round 4 (Right Side) Chain 1, *single crochet in each stitch across to next corner, 2 single crochet in corner chain 1-space; repeat from * around. Join with slip stitch in first single crochet—11 single crochet on each side. Fasten off B.

SQUARE 2—MAKE 2

With B, chain 4. Join with slip stitch to form ring.

Round 1 (Right Side) Chain 3, 2 double crochet in ring, chain 1, [3 double crochet, chain 1] 3 times in ring. Join with slip stitch in top of beginning chain. Turn—4 corner chain 1-spaces.

Round 2 (Wrong Side) Slip stitch in first chain 1-space, chain 3, double crochet in same chain 1-space, *double crochet in each of next 3 double crochet, [2 double crochet, chain 1, 2 double crochet] in next corner chain 1-space; repeat from * around, ending with 2 double crochet in first chain 1-space already holding 1 double crochet, chain 1. Join with slip stitch in top of beginning chain. Turn—4 corner chain 1-spaces; 7 double crochet on each side.

Round 3 (Right Side) Slip stitch in first corner chain 1-space, chain 3, double crochet in same chain 1-space, *double crochet in each double crochet across to next corner, [2 double crochet, chain 1, 2 double crochet] in next corner chain 1-space; repeat from * around, ending with 2 double crochet in first chain 1-space already holding 1 double crochet, chain 1. Join with slip stitch top of beginning chain—4 corner chain 1-spaces; 11 double crochet on each side.

Round 4 (Right Side) Chain 1, *single crochet in each stitch across to next corner, 2 single crochet in corner chain 1-space; repeat from * around. Join with slip stitch in first single crochet—13 single crochet on each side. Fasten off.

SQUARE 3—MAKE 4

With A, chain 6. Join with slip stitch to form ring.

Round 1 (Right Side) Chain 3, work 15 double crochet in ring. Join with slip stitch in top of beginning chain. Turn—16 stitches.

Round 2 (Wrong Side) Chain 4, skip first double crochet, [double crochet, chain 1] in each double crochet around. Join with slip stitch in 3rd chain of beginning chain. Turn—16 chain 1-spaces.

Round 3 (Right Side) Slip stitch in first chain 1-space, chain 3, double crochet in same chain 1-space, *2 double crochet in each of next 3 chain 1-spaces, [2 double crochet, chain 1, 2 double crochet] in next chain 1-space; repeat from * around, ending with 2 double crochet in first chain 1-space already holding 1 double crochet, chain 1. Join with slip stitch in top of beginning chain—4 corner chain 1-spaces.

Round 4 (Right Side) Chain 1, *single crochet in each stitch across to next corner, 2 single crochet in corner chain 1-space; repeat from * around. Join with slip stitch in first single crochet—12 single crochet on each side. Fasten off.

SQUARE 4—MAKE 2

With A, chain 6. Join with slip stitch to form ring.

Round 1 (Right Side) Chain 1, [single crochet, chain 3] 8 times in ring. Join with slip stitch in first single crochet—8 chain 3-spaces.

Round 2 Chain 4, working behind chain 3-spaces of Round 1, *single crochet in ring between next 2 single crochet, chain 4; repeat from * 6 more times, ending with slip stitch in ring between last single crochet and first single crochet—8 chain 4-loops.

Round 3 [single crochet, chain 1, 2 double crochet, chain 1, slip stitch] in each chain 4-loop around. Join with slip stitch in first single crochet—8 petals.

Round 4 Working behind petals of Round 3, chain 4, *single crochet around the post of next corresponding single crochet 2 rounds below, chain 4; repeat from * 6 more times. Join with slip stitch in first chain 4-loop—8 chain 4-loops.

Round 5 Chain 3, [2 double crochet, chain 2, 3 double crochet] in same loop, 3 double crochet in next chain 4-loop, *[3 double crochet, chain 2, 3 double crochet] in next chain 4-loop, 3 double crochet in next chain 4-loop; repeat from * around. Join with slip stitch in top of beginning chain—4 corner chain 2-spaces; 9 double crochet on each side. Fasten off.

SQUARE 5—MAKE 4

With A, chain 6. Join with slip stitch to form ring.

Round 1 (Right Side) Chain 1, work 16 single crochet in ring. Join with slip stitch in first single crochet. Turn—16 single crochet.

Round 2 (Wrong Side) Chain 3, [double crochet, chain 1, 2 double crochet] in same stitch, skip next single crochet, *[2 double crochet, chain 1, 2 double crochet] in next single crochet, skip next single crochet; repeat from * around. Join with slip stitch in top of beginning chain. Turn—8 chain 1-spaces.

Round 3 (Right Side) Chain 3, 2 double crochet in same chain 1-space, *chain 1, 3 double crochet in next chain 1-space, chain 1, [3 double crochet, chain 1, 3 double crochet] in next chain 1-space; repeat from * around, ending with 3 double crochet in first chain 1-space already holding 2 double crochet, chain 1. Join with slip stitch in top of beginning ch—4 corner chain 1-spaces; 2 chain 1-spaces; 9 double crochet on each side.

Round 4 (Right Side) Chain 1, *single crochet in each double crochet across to next corner, 2 single crochet in corner chain 1-space; repeat from * around. Join with slip stitch in first single crochet—11 single crochet on each side. Fasten off.

ASSEMBLY

Weave in ends. Put Squares in your washer and fill with a couple of inches of cool water. Thoroughly wet Squares by gently squeezing in the water. Spin briefly until just damp. Lay the damp Squares on a towel and gently ease them into shape, blocking to size, pinning where necessary. Allow to dry completely.

With wrong side facing and C, following same construction diagram for Front and Back, join Squares on bottom row to Squares in 2nd row by working a row of single crochet through both thicknesses in back loops only of stitches. Then join top 2 Squares to corresponding Squares of 2nd row in same manner. In same manner, join vertical strips to each other for Front and Back.

GUSSET

Row 1 With right side of Back facing, join A in back loop of top left corner stitch. Working across left side edge, chain 3, double crochet in back loop of each stitch down side, across bottom, and up other side edge to top right corner stitch. Turn.

Row 2 Chain 1, single crochet in each double crochet across to top left corner. Fasten off A.

Row 3 (Joining Row) With wrong sides of Front and Back facing, working through both loops of stitches in last row of Gusset and through front loops only of stitches in outer edge of Front, chain 1, single crochet in each stitch across side, bottom and other side edge. Fasten off. Weave in ends.

FINISHING

Outer Trim (Handle Joining Round) With right side of Front facing, join C in top right corner of top left Square on Front. Holding left side of one handle over stitches on top edge, chain 1, working over handle, single crochet in each stitch across top edge of Square; working across side edge of Front, working in remaining front loops of stitches on Front, single crochet in each stitch down left side, across bottom and up right side edge; working over other end of same handle, single crochet in each stitch across top edge of top right Square; working in back loops of stitches, single crochet in each stitch across left side of same Square, across top of center Square and across right side of top left Square. Join with slip stitch in first single crochet. Fasten off.

Repeat Outer Trim on Back, joining other handle. Weave in ends.

With sewing needle and thread, sew one shell to center of each Square 1 and Square 4 on Front and Back.

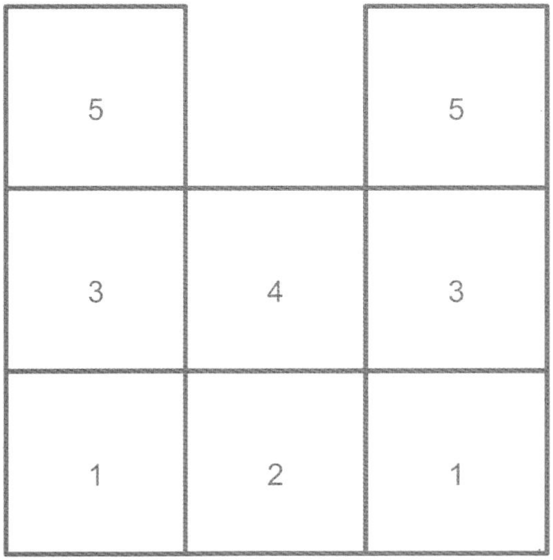

5		5
3	4	3
1	2	1

Assembly Diagram

STRIPE IT RICH

DESIGNED BY STEPHANIE KLOSE

CROCHET/BEGINNER

This cheerful striped bag is a simple rectangle. The shaping at the top comes from cinching the fabric around the handles.

SIZE

12" wide x 14" tall (30.5 x 35.5 cm), plus Handles

MATERIALS

LION BRAND HOMESPUN
98% ACRYLIC, 2% POLYESTER
6 OZ (170 G) 185 YD (167 M)
SKEIN

1 skein each #386 Grape (A), #390 Lavender Sachet (B), #385 Fuchsia (C) or colors of your choice

- Size K-10.5 (6.5 mm) crochet hook *or size to obtain gauge*
- Two circular handles 12" (30.5 cm) wide
- Large-eyed, blunt needle

GAUGE

13 single crochets + 12 rows = 4" (10 cm).
Be sure to check your gauge.

BACK

With A, chain 39.

Row 1 (Right Side) Single crochet in 2nd chain from hook and in each chain across. Turn—38 single crochet.

Row 2 Chain 1, single crochet in each single crochet across. Turn.

Continue in single crochet in the following color sequence: 4 more rows A; 6 rows B; 6 rows C; 6 rows A; 6 rows B; 6 rows C; 12 rows A (Bottom); 6 rows C; 6 rows B; 6 rows A; 6 rows C; 6 rows B; 6 rows A.

Do not fasten off.

FRONT HANDLE CASING

Row 1 Chain 4, skip first single crochet, double crochet in next single crochet, *chain 1, skip next single crochet, double crochet in next single crochet; repeat from * across—19 chain 1-spaces. Fasten off.

BACK HANDLE CASING

Row 1 With right side facing, working across opposite side of foundation chain, join A in first chain, chain 4, skip first chain, double crochet in next chain, *chain 1, skip next chain, double crochet in next chain; repeat from * across—19 chain 1-spaces. Fasten off.

FINISHING

Fold Handle casing to wrong side over bottom of circular handle. With large-eyed, blunt needle, sew Handle casing to inside of Bag. Repeat on other side of Bag. With right side of front and back facing, sew side seams, matching yarn to stripe color. Weave in ends. Turn Bag right side out.

SILVER LINING

DESIGNED BY LORNA MISER

KNIT/EASY

The classic tote gets a makeover when knitted side to side in a cool palette of silvery grays.

SIZE

15" wide x 16" tall (38 x 40.5 cm), excluding Handles

MATERIALS

LION BRAND COLOR WAVES
83% ACRYLIC, 17% POLYESTER
3 OZ (85 G) 125 YD (113 M) SKEIN

1 skein #350 Night Sky (A) or color of your choice

LION BRAND WOOL-EASE
80% ACRYLIC, 20% WOOL
3 OZ (85 G) 197 YD (180 M) BALL

1 ball each #152 Oxford Grey (B)
#151 Grey Heather (C)
#501 White Frost (D) or colors of your choice

LION BRAND GLITTERSPUN
60% ACRYLIC, 13% POLYESTER,
27% CUPRO 1¾ OZ (50 G) 115 YD (105 M) BALL

1 ball #150 Silver (E) or color of your choice

LION BRAND MOONLIGHT MOHAIR
MOONLIGHT MOHAIR
35% MOHAIR, 30% ACRYLIC, 25% COTTON, 10% METALLIC POLYESTER
1≤ OZ (50 G) 82 YD (75 M) BALL

1 ball #202 Tundra (F) or color of your choice

- Size 7 (4.5 mm) knitting needles *or size to obtain gauge*
- ½ yard (0.5 m) cotton fabric
- Therm O Web Heat 'n' Bond fusible adhesive
- Iron
- Large-eyed, blunt needle
- Somerset Designs black suede handles
- Black sewing thread

GAUGE

16 stitches + 26 rows = 4" (10 cm) in stockinette stitch (knit on right side, purl on wrong side) with B.
Be sure to check your gauge.

STRIPE SEQUENCE

2 rows B; 4 rows E; 8 rows A; 2 rows C; 4 rows D; 8 rows F.

PURSE

With B, cast on 66 stitches. Work in stockinette stitch, following Stripe Sequence, until piece measures 30" (76 cm) from beginning. Bind off all stitches.

ASSEMBLY

Cut a 16" x 30" (40.5 x 76 cm) rectangle of Heat 'n' Bond. Fuse to wrong side of cotton fabric. Trim excess fabric. Peel off paper. Lay knit piece right side down on ironing surface. Place adhesive side of fabric onto Purse. Line up all edges and fuse in place, using low temperature only and no steam. Sew side and bottom seams of Purse. **Optional** Fuse 1" (2.5 cm) strips of fabric over seams on the inside of Purse.

Determine placement of suede handles and pin in place. Use doubled sewing thread to sew through precut holes.

To form base of Purse, fold the bottom corners to the inside, making small triangles on the inside of the Purse. Press or stitch in place.

GET A HANDLE ON IT

DESIGNED BY DORIS CHAN

CROCHET/INTERMEDIATE

Use your imagination! Handles can be created from a variety of everyday objects. Cut out the centers from a pair of plastic lids and crochet around them for custom handles.

SIZE

12" wide x 6" tall (30.5 x 15 cm), excluding Handles

MATERIALS

LION BRAND COLOR WAVES
83% ACRYLIC, 17% POLYESTER
3 OZ (85 G) 125 YD (113 M) SKEIN

1 skein #398 Pebble Beach (A) or color of your choice

LION BRAND WOOL-EASE
80% ACRYLIC, 20% WOOL
3 OZ (85 G) 197 YD (180 M) BALL

1 ball #147 Purple (B) or color of your choice

- Size K-10.5 (6.5 mm) crochet hook *or size to obtain gauge*
- Scraps of contrasting yarn to be used as markers
- Two plastic container lids, 6" (15 cm) in diameter, or any similar lids
- Sharp scissors (curved nail scissors are perfect)
- Emery board or sandpaper
- Large-eyed, blunt needle

GAUGE

12 single crochet + 13 rows = 4" (10 cm) with A.
Be sure to check your gauge.

NOTE

Bag begins with a Square motif, worked in stripes, back and forth in the round. This Square will eventually be folded diagonally in half to form the bottom fold, with striped triangles forming Front and Back of Bag. The two shaped Side Triangles are worked onto the Square. Handles are sewn on later.

HANDLES

Prepare plastic lids for Handles. Start with 2 clean, dry lids. Using scissors, carefully cut out and remove the flat center part of lid, leaving a ¼" (6 mm)-wide inner ridge and ¼" (6 mm)-deep outer rim (the part that snaps over the edge of the container). Sand away any rough spots. The resulting ring is 6" (15 cm) in diameter. It does not matter which side of the lid faces you as you are working; just do the 2nd Handle with the same side facing. The covered ring will have a flat side and a bumpy side. Try to rotate and ease the single crochet stitches so that the right side of the single crochet is also the bumpy side. This helps the Handles to lie flatter against each other when attached.

Round 1 With 2 strands of B held together, join yarn in one prepared ring, chain 1, single crochet closely and evenly spaced around ring, approximately 100 single crochet. Join with slip stitch in first single crochet. Fasten off, leaving an 18" (45.5 cm) long tail for sewing. Weave in ends.

Repeat Round 1 for 2nd prepared ring.

SQUARE

With A, chain 2.

Round 1 (Right Side) 4 single crochet in 2nd chain from hook. Join with slip stitch in first single crochet. Turn—4 single crochet.

Round 2 (Wrong Side) Chain 1, 2 single crochet in each single crochet around. Join with slip stitch in first single crochet. Turn—8 single crochet.

Round 3 (Right Side) Chain 1, *single crochet in next single crochet, 3 single crochet in next single crochet, place a marker in middle single crochet; repeat from * 3 more times. Join with slip stitch in first single crochet. Turn—16 single crochet.

Note Move markers up as work progresses.

Round 4 (Wrong Side) Chain 1, *single crochet in each single crochet to next marker, 3 single crochet in marked single crochet; repeat from * around, single crochet in each single crochet to beginning. Join with slip stitch in first single crochet. Turn—24 single crochet. Fasten off A.

Round 5 (Right Side) With 2 strands of B held together, join yarn in first single crochet, repeat Round 4—32 single crochet.

Round 6 (Wrong Side) Repeat Round 4—40 single crochet. Fasten off B. Join A.

Rounds 7–14 Repeat Round 4 in the following color sequence: *2 rounds A; 2 rounds with 2 strands of B held together; repeat from * once—104 single crochet at end of Round 14. Fasten off.

FIRST SIDE TRIANGLE

Note Beginning at one corner of the Square, each Side Triangle is worked onto 2 edges of the Square. The piece "bounces" back and forth, alternately joined to one edge, then the other edge of the Square as you go.

Row 1 (Right Side) With right side of Square facing, join A in single crochet before any marked corner single crochet, chain 1, 3 single crochet in marked single crochet, slip stitch in next 2 single crochet of Square. Turn—3 single crochet.

Row 2 Skip slip stitches, 2 single crochet in next single crochet, single crochet in next single crochet and place marker, 2 single crochet in next single crochet, slip stitch in next 2 single crochet of Square. Turn—5 single crochet.

Row 3 Skip slip stitches, single crochet in next single crochet, 2 single crochet in next single crochet, single crochet in marked single crochet, 2 single crochet in next single crochet, single crochet in next single crochet, slip stitch in next 2 single crochet of Square. Turn—7 single crochet.

Row 4 Skip slip stitches, single crochet in each single crochet across until 1 single crochet remains before marked stitch, 2 single crochet in single crochet before marker, single crochet in marked stitch, 2 single crochet in single crochet after marker, single crochet in each single crochet across, slip stitch in next 2 single crochet of Square. Turn—9 single crochet.

Rows 5–9 Repeat Row 4—19 single crochet at end of Row 9.

Row 10 Skip slip stitches, single crochet in each single crochet across, slip stitch in next 2 single crochet of Square. Turn—19 single crochet.

Rows 11–20 Repeat Rows 9–10—29 single crochet at end of Row 20.

Rows 21–26 Repeat Row 10—29 single crochet.

Fasten off.

SECOND SIDE TRIANGLE

Work Second Side Triangle as for First Side Triangle, starting at opposite corner of Square. Weave in ends.

TOP EDGING

Round 1 With right side of Bag facing, with 2 strands of B held together, join yarn in top marked center single crochet of top corner of Square, chain 1, single crochet in same single crochet, single crochet in each single crochet across top edge of Side, single crochet in marked center single crochet of other top corner of Square, single crochet in each single crochet across top edge of Side. Join with slip stitch in first single crochet. Turn—60 single crochet.

Round 2 Chain 1, single crochet in each single crochet around. Join with slip stitch in first single crochet. Fasten off.

Place a marker in stitch at center of each side of bag.

ATTACH HANDLES

Hold Bag and Handle with right side facing. Skip marked single crochet at center of one side of bag, skip next 4 single crochet on top edge of Side. With large-eyed, blunt needle and tail, *insert needle in next single crochet of Bag (under 2 loops as if to crochet), sew to next single crochet of Handle, insert needle in same single crochet of bag, sew to next single crochet of Handle; repeat from * 20 more times. Fasten off, leaving last 4 single crochet on top edge of Side free.

Attach other Handle on opposite side of Bag in same manner. Weave in ends.

3.

COLOR BY DAY

Classic and reliable styles like messenger bags and totes make a good background for color-work techniques like patchwork knitting, intarsia, and eye-catching granny squares. Experiment with different palettes and textures. You'll find your road to self-expression and make some gorgeous bags along the way.

MAKING A GRANNY SQUARE

Granny squares are simple geometric shapes, making them perfect building blocks for a bag. Or they can be used as single motifs for a colorful accent. Using single or multiple colors, granny squares are portable projects, allowing you to satisfy your stitching needs on the go. Consider the open quality of granny squares and think about lining your bag or embellishing the centers with beads or buttons.

Forming a ring is the first step. Chain as many stitches as the pattern dictates, insert the hook into the first chain above the slip knot (illustration 1), yarn over the hook and pull through the first chain and the chain on the hook (illustration 2).

Working into the ring (or under the chain): After you have created the ring, chain 3 chains if you are using double crochet, yarn over and insert the hook under the ring, yarn over and pull up a stitch. When you are working your third or larger rounds, make sure you insert your hook completely underneath the chain below it (illustration 3).

A handy tip when you begin each round is to hold the tail yarn on top of the chain you are crocheting into and crochet the tail so that it is tucked into the chain. This secures the ends as you work, making it easier to weave them later. It is a good idea to weave in your ends as you go so you won't be faced with dozens of ends when you are done crocheting your project and are anxious to show it off.

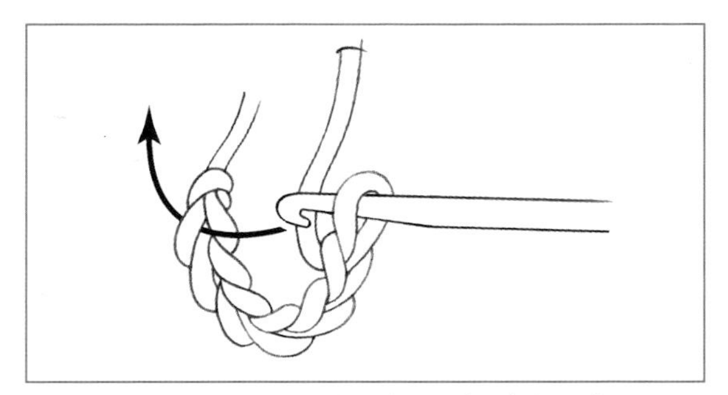

1. Joining granny square ring: insert hook into first chain stitch.

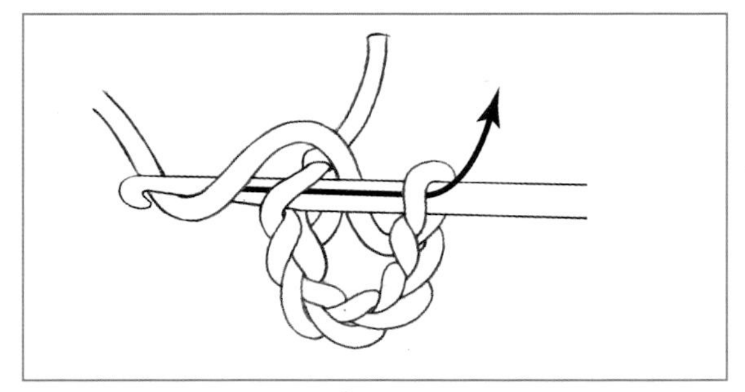

2. Yarn over, pull through chain and stitch on hook.

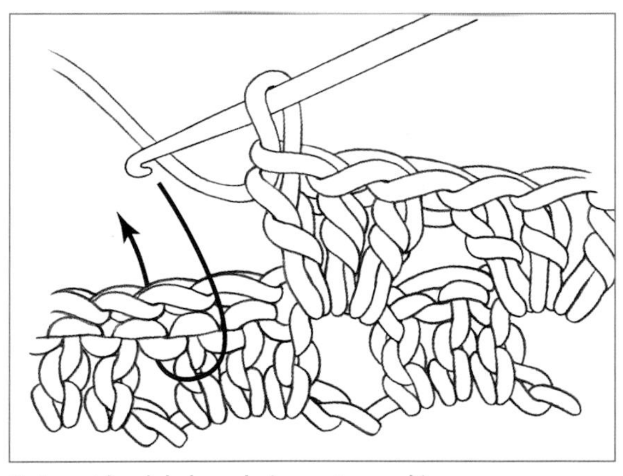

3. Insert hook below chain you're working on.

GRANNY ON THE GO

DESIGNED BY KATHERINE ENG

CROCHET/INTERMEDIATE

Whip up this fun handbag in no time—it's just two big granny squares.

SIZE

10½" wide x 10½" tall (26.5 x 26.5 cm), excluding Strap

MATERIALS

LION BRAND CHENILLE THICK & QUICK 91% ACRYLIC, 9% RAYON 100 YD (90 M) SKEIN

1 skein each #189 Wine (A) #098 Antique White (B) or colors of your choice

LION BRAND HOMESPUN 98% ACRYLIC, 2% POLYESTER 6 OZ (170 G) 185 YD (169 M) SKEIN

1 skein #312 Edwardian (C) or color of your choice

- Size H-8 (5 mm) crochet hook *or size to obtain gauge*
- One 1³⁄₁₆" (3 cm) gray button
- Large-eyed, blunt needle

GAUGE

Round 1 of Square = 2½" (6.5 cm) across.
Square = 10½" x 10½" (26.5 x 26.5 cm).
Be sure to check your gauge.

STITCH EXPLANATIONS

FPdc (front post double crochet) Yarn over, working from front to back to front, insert hook around post of stitch of row below, yarn over and draw up a loop, (yarn over and draw through 2 loops on hook) twice. Skip stitch behind the FPdc.
Shell 5 double crochet in same stitch.

FRONT SQUARE

With B, chain 4. Join with slip stitch to form ring.
Round 1 (Right Side) Chain 3, 2 double crochet in ring, chain 2, [3 double crochet, chain 2] 3 times in ring. Join with slip stitch in top of beginning chain—4 corner chain 2-spaces. Fasten off B.
Round 2 With right side facing, join C in corner chain 2-space, chain 1, *[single crochet, chain 2, single crochet] in chain 2-space, chain 1, skip next double crochet, 2 FPdc around the post of next double crochet, chain 1, skip next dc; repeat from * around. Join with slip stitch in first single crochet. Turn—4 corner chain 2-spaces.
Round 3 (Wrong Side) Chain 1, *single crochet in next chain 1-space, chain 1, 3 double crochet in next FPdc, chain 2, 3 double crochet in next FPdc, chain 1, single crochet in next chain 1-space, chain 1, slip stitch in next chain 2-space, chain 1; repeat from * around. Join with slip stitch in first single crochet. Turn—4 corner chain 2-spaces.
Round 4 (Right Side) Chain 1, *single crochet in chain 1-space, chain

1, skip next slip stitch, single crochet in next chain 1-space, single crochet in next single crochet, single crochet in next chain 1-space, single crochet in each of next 2 double crochet, [single crochet, chain 2, single crochet] in chain 2-space, skip next double crochet, single crochet in each of next 2 double crochet, single crochet in next chain 1-space, single crochet in next single crochet; repeat from * around. Join with slip stitch in first single crochet—4 corner chain 2-spaces; [6 single crochet, chain 1, 6 single crochet] on each side. Fasten off C.

Round 5 With right side facing, join A in any chain 1-space on side of Front Square, chain 1, *single crochet in chain 1-space, chain 1, skip next 2 single crochet, single crochet in next single crochet, chain 1, skip next single crochet, single crochet in next single crochet, chain 1, skip next single crochet, [single crochet, chain 2, single crochet] in next corner chain 2-space, [chain 1, skip next single crochet, single crochet in next single crochet] twice, chain 1, skip next 2 single crochet; repeat from * around. Join with slip stitch in first sc—4 corner chain 2-spaces; 6 chain 1-spaces on each side.

Round 6 Chain 3, 2 double crochet in same single crochet, **skip next chain 1-space, single crochet in next single crochet, *skip next chain 1-space, 3 double crochet in next single crochet, skip next chain 1-space, single crochet in next sc*, [2 double crochet, chain 2, 2 double crochet] in next chain 2-space, single crochet in next single crochet; repeat from * to * once, skip next chain 1-space, 3 double crochet in next single crochet; repeat from ** around, omitting last 3 double crochet. Join with slip stitch in top of beginning chain—4 corner chain 2-spaces. Fasten off A.

Round 7 With right side facing, join B in first double crochet to the left of any corner chain 2-space, chain 1, **single crochet in double crochet, *chain 1, skip next double crochet, double crochet in next single crochet, chain 1, skip next double crochet, single crochet in next dc; repeat from * across to next corner, chain 1 (single crochet, chain 2, single crochet) in corner chain 2-space, chain 1; repeat from ** around—4 corner chain 2-spaces; 10 chain 1-spaces on each side. Fasten off B.

Round 8 With right side facing, join C in first chain 1-space to the left of any corner chain 2-space, chain 1, *single crochet in each space and stitch across to next corner, [single-crochet, chain 2, single crochet] in corner chain 2-space, single crochet in next single crochet; repeat from * around. Join with slip stitch in first single crochet—4 corner chain 2-spaces; 23 single crochet on each side.

Round 9 Chain 1, **single crochet in single crochet, skip next 2 single crochet, *shell in next single crochet, skip next 2 single crochet, single crochet in next single crochet, skip next 2 single crochet; repeat from * across to next corner, 7 double crochet in next corner chain 2-space, skip next 2 single crochet; repeat from ** around. Join with slip stitch in first single crochet—3 shells on each side.

Round 10 Chain 1, **single crochet in single crochet, chain 2, *skip next 2 double crochet, [single crochet, chain 2, single crochet] in next double crochet, chain 2, skip next 2 double crochet, [single crochet, chain 2, single crochet] in next single crochet; repeat from * across to next corner, skip next 2 double crochet, [single crochet, chain 2, single crochet] in next double crochet, [single crochet, chain 4, single crochet] in next double crochet, [single crochet, chain 2, single crochet] in next double crochet, skip next 2 double crochet; repeat from ** around. Join with slip stitch in first single crochet—4 corner chain 4-loops; 12 chain 2-spaces on each side. Fasten off.

BACK SQUARE

Work as for Front Square through Round 9. Mark position for button loop in center double crochet of center shell on top edge of Back.

Round 10 With wrong side of Front and Back facing, work as for Round 10 of Front, joining Back to Front in each chain 4-loop and each chain 2-space on 3 sides as follows: To join chain 4-loops, work single crochet in corner double crochet, chain 2, drop loop from hook, insert hook from front to back in corresponding chain 4-loop of Front, pick up dropped loop, chain 2, single crochet in same double crochet of Back; to join chain 2-spaces, work single crochet in double crochet, chain 1, drop loop from hook, insert hook from front to back in corresponding chain 2-space of Front, pick up dropped loop, chain 1, single crochet in same double crochet of Back; at marker on center double crochet at top edge of Back, work [single crochet, chain 14, slip stitch in 2nd chain from hook, chain 12, single crochet] in marked double crochet. After completing Round 10, fasten off.

STRAP

With 2 strands of C held together, chain 100.

Round 1 Single crochet in 2nd chain from hook and in each chain across to last chain, 3 single crochet in last chain; working across opposite side of foundation chain, single crochet in each chain across to last chain, 2 single crochet in last chain. Join with slip stitch in first single crochet. Fasten off, leaving a tail for sewing.

FINISHING

With large-eyed, blunt needle and tail, with right side facing out, sew one end of Strap to inside of Bag at one side seam. Without twisting Strap, sew other end of Strap to inside at opposite side of Bag. Sew button onto Front below button loop. Weave in ends.

INTARSIA TOTE

DESIGNED BY STEPHANIE KLOSE

KNIT/EASY

This bag is the perfect introduction to intarsia. The self-patterning yarn used in the intarsia block makes it look more complicated than it is.

SIZE

10" wide x 12" long x 2" deep (25.5 x 30.5 x 5 cm), approximately, excluding Strap

MATERIALS

LION BRAND WOOL-EASE
80% ACRYLIC, 20% WOOL
3 OZ (85 G) 197 YD (180 M) BALL

1 ball #153 Black (A) or color of your choice

LION BRAND MAGIC STRIPES
75% SUPERWASH WOOL, 25% NYLON 3½ OZ (100G) 330 YD (300M) BALL

1 ball #206 Lumberjack Black (B) or color of your choice

- Size 7 (4.5 mm) knitting needles *or size to obtain gauge*
- Scraps of contrasting yarn to be used as markers
- Large snap
- Sewing needle and matching thread
- Large-eyed, blunt needle

GAUGE

18 stitches + 24 rows = 4" (10 cm) in stockinette stitch (knit on right side, purl on wrong side) with A.
Be sure to check your gauge.

PATTERN STITCH

Seed stitch (odd number of stitches)
Row 1 Knit 1, [purl 1, knit 1] across.
Repeat Row 1 for pattern.

BAG

With A, cast on 45 stitches. Work in seed stitch for 1" (2.5 cm). Change to stockinette stitch and work even until piece measures 3½" (9 cm) from beginning.

INTARSIA SECTION

Note Use both ends of yarn ball. Twist yarns at color changes to prevent holes.
Row 1 Continuing in stockinette stitch, work 12 stitches with A, 21 stitches with 2 strands of B held together, 12 stitches with A.
Repeat Row 1 for 6" (15 cm). Cut both strands of B.
With A only, work 1½" (4 cm) in stockinette stitch. Mark both ends of last row for Strap placement. Work 2" (5 cm) in stockinette stitch. Mark both ends of last row for Strap placement. Work in stockinette stitch for 11" (28 cm). Work in seed stitch for 1" (2.5 cm). Bind off all stitches.

STRAP

With A, cast on 9 stitches. Work in seed stitch for 40" (101.5 cm). Bind off.

FINISHING

Sew short ends of Strap to Bag between markers on both sides. Sew side edges of Strap to front and back of Bag. Weave in ends. Sew snap to Bag opening.

TUTTI FRUTTI BAG

DESIGNED BY DORIS CHAN

CROCHET/INTERMEDIATE

Dress up this easy bag with a bunch of fun-to-crochet grapes.

SIZE

13" wide x 6½" tall [33 x 16.5 cm), excluding Strap

MATERIALS

LION BRAND COLOR WAVES
83% ACRYLIC, 17% POLYESTER
3 OZ (85 G) 125 YD (114 M) SKEIN

2 skeins #341 Mai Tai (MC) or color of your choice

LION BRAND LION SUEDE
100% POLYESTER 3 OZS (85 G)
122 YARDS (110 M) BALL

1 ball #146 Fuchsia (CC) or color of your choice

- Size K-10.5 (6.5 mm) crochet hook *or size to obtain gauge*
- Scraps of contrasting yarn to be used as markers
- Large-eyed, blunt needle

GAUGE

9.5 single crochet + 11 rows = 4" (10 cm) with MC.
Be sure to check your gauge.

STITCH EXPLANATIONS

sc2tog (single crochet decrease) Insert hook into stitch and draw up a loop. Insert hook into next stitch and draw up a loop. Yarn over, draw through all 3 loops on hook.
Cluster [Yarn over, insert hook in same stitch and draw up a loop, yarn over and draw through 2 loops] 3 times in same stitch, yarn over, draw through all loops on hook.

RING—MAKE 2

With CC, chain 8. Join with slip stitch to form ring.
Round 1 Chain 1, work 20 single crochet in ring. Join with slip stitch in first single crochet—20 single crochet. Fasten off.

BODY

With MC, chain 23.
Round 1 (Wrong Side) 2 single crochet in 2nd chain from hook, single crochet in next 20 chain, 4 single crochet in last chain; working on opposite side of foundation chain, single crochet in next 20 chain, 2 single crochet in last chain. Join with slip stitch in first single crochet. Turn—48 single crochet.
Round 2 (Right Side) Chain 1, single crochet in first single crochet (place a marker in this single crochet for center of side), 2 single crochet in next single crochet, single crochet in next 20 single crochet, 2 single crochet in next single crochet, single crochet in next 2 single crochet (place a marker in these 2 single crochet), 2 single crochet in next single crochet, single crochet in next 20 single crochet, 2 single crochet in next single crochet, single crochet in last single crochet (place a marker in this single crochet for center of side). Join with slip stitch in first single crochet. Turn—52 single crochet.
Note Move all markers up as work progresses.

Round 3 (Wrong Side) Chain 1, single crochet in first single crochet, 2 single crochet in next single crochet, single crochet in each single crochet across to first stitch before marked stitches, 2 single crochet in next single crochet, single crochet in next 2 marked single crochet, 2 single crochet in next single crochet, single crochet in each single crochet across to first stitch before marked stitch, 2 single crochet in next single crochet, single crochet in last single crochet. Join with slip stitch in first single crochet. Turn—56 single crochet.

Rounds 4–5 Repeat Round 3, increasing 4 single crochet in each round as established—64 single crochet at end of Round 5.

Rounds 6–19 Chain 1, single crochet in each single crochet around, continuing to move markers up as work progresses. Join with slip stitch in first single crochet. Turn. Fasten off.

Note Next round shifts the join forward 3 stitches. It also creates holes for the rings, drops the rings in place, and encloses them in one step. To work through center of Ring, not around Ring, hold hook and feeder yarn above work, dip hook through Ring to insert in single crochet, yarn over, keeping feeder yarn above and in front of Ring, draw up a loop, complete single crochet.

Round 20 (Right Side) With right side facing, skip first 3 single crochet, join MC in next single crochet, chain 1, single crochet in same single crochet, single crochet in next 25 single crochet, chain 1, *with right side of Ring and Bag facing, lay Ring across top of next few stitches, skip next single crochet; working through Ring, single crochet in each of next 4 single crochet, chain 1, skip next single crochet *, single crochet in next 26 single crochet, chain 1; repeat from * to * to join 2nd Ring. Join with slip stitch in first single crochet. Turn—60 single crochet; 4 chain 1-spaces.

Round 21 Chain 1, single crochet in each single crochet and in each chain 1-space around. Join with slip stitch in first single crochet. Turn—64 single crochet.

Round 22 Chain 1, *single crochet in next 6 single crochet, single crochet 2 together in next 2 stitches; repeat from * around. Join with slip stitch in first single crochet. Turn—56 single crochet.

Rounds 23–29 Chain 1, single crochet in each single crochet around. Join with slip stitch in first single crochet. Turn.
Fasten off MC.

Round 30 With right side facing, join CC in any single crochet, chain 1, single crochet in each single crochet around. Join with slip stitch in first single crochet. Turn.

Round 31 chain 1, single crochet in each single crochet around. Join with slip stitch in first single crochet. Turn. Fasten off.

STRAP

With CC, chain 80.

Row 1 Single crochet in 2nd chain from hook and in each chain across. Turn—79 single crochet.

Row 2 Chain 4, *skip next single crochet, cluster in next single crochet, chain 1; repeat from * across to last 2 stitches, skip next single crochet, double crochet in last single crochet. Turn—38 clusters.

Row 3 Chain 1, single crochet in first double crochet, *single crochet in next chain 1-space, single crochet in next cluster; repeat from * across to last chain 1-space, single crochet in last chain 1-space, single crochet in 3rd chain of turning chain. Fasten off CC, leaving a tail for sewing.

With large-eyed, blunt needle and CC, sew ends of Strap to center 5 single crochet of ring on each side of bag, being careful not to twist Strap. Weave in ends.

GRAPES—MAKE 9

With CC, leaving a long tail, chain 2.

Round 1 8 single crochet in 2nd chain from hook. Do not join. Work in a spiral, placing a marker in first stitch and moving marker up as work progresses—8 single crochet.

Rounds 2–5 Single crochet in each single crochet around.

Fasten off, leaving a long tail for sewing.

Stuff beginning tail into Grape. Thread ending tail on needle, weave in and out of last round, pull up gently to gather top of Grape, secure, and stuff end into Grape.

STEM

With CC, chain 14. Slip stitch in 2nd chain from hook, slip stitch in top of one Grape, slip stitch in next 2 chain of Stem, chain 3, slip stitch in top of next Grape, slip stitch in first 2 chain of ch-3, chain 2, slip stitch in top of next Grape, slip stitch in each chain of ch-2, slip stitch in skipped chain of previous chain-3, slip stitch in next 3 chain of Stem, *ch 3, slip stitch in top of next Grape, slip stitch in first 2 chain of ch-3, chain 3, slip stitch in top of next Grape, slip stitch in first 2 chain of ch-3, chain 2, slip stitch in top of next Grape, slip stitch in each chain of chain-2, slip stitch in skipped chain of previous ch-3, slip stitch in skipped chain of previous ch-3, slip stitch in next 3 chain of Stem chain; repeat from * once, slip stitch in last chain of Stem. Fasten off. Weave in ends.

Fold over 4" (10 cm) of Bag (from Ring to Ring) for Flap. Tack bunch of Grapes along Stem at a couple of places to front of Flap or where desired.

LOG CABIN TOTE

DESIGNED BY LORNA MISER

KNIT/EASY

A great way to mix color, patchwork knitting starts with a center motif and works its way out with picked-up stitches. Changing color every time you work a new section helps keep track of the pattern.

SIZE

Approximately 12" tall x 12" wide x 2" deep (30.5 x 30.5 x 5 cm), excluding Handle

MATERIALS

LION BRAND LION SUEDE
100% POLYESTER 3 OZS (85 G)
122 YARDS (110 M) BALL

1 ball each #133 Spice (A)
#132 Olive (B)
#146 Fuchsia (C)
#178 Teal (D)
#147 Eggplant (E) or colors of your choice

- Size 7 (4.5 mm) knitting needles *or size to obtain gauge*
- ½ yd (½ m) cotton quilting fabric to coordinate for lining
- 1 yard (1 m) Ultra Bond fusible adhesive
- Iron
- Large-eyed, blunt needle

GAUGE

14 stitches + 28 rows = 4" (10 cm) in garter stitch (knit every row).
Be sure to check your gauge.

SQUARES—MAKE 8

With A, cast on 4 stitches. Knit 8 rows. Bind off.

With right side facing and B, pick up and knit 4 stitches along side edge of square, beginning in last cast-on stitch of A and picking up 1 stitch in each ridge. Knit 8 rows. Bind off, leaving last stitch on needle and do not break yarn. Turn work clockwise. Count stitch on needle as first stitch, pick up and knit 3 more stitches along edge of B square and 4 stitches along bound-off edge of A square—8 stitches. Knit 8 rows. Bind off and break yarn. Turn work clockwise.

With right side facing and C, pick up and knit 8 stitches along edge, beginning in last bound-off stitch of B. Knit 8 rows. Bind off, leaving last stitch on needle and do not break yarn. Turn work clockwise, pick up and knit 11 more stitches from next edge—12 stitches. Knit 8 rows. Bind off and break yarn. Turn work clockwise.

With right side facing and D, pick up and knit 12 stitches along next edge, begin in last bound-off stitch of C. Knit 8 rows. Bind off, leaving last stitch on needle and do not break yarn. Turn work clockwise, pick up and knit 15 more stitches from next edge—16 stitches. Knit 8 rows. Bind off and break yarn. Turn work clockwise.

With right side facing and E, pick up and knit 16 stitches along next edge, begin in last bound-off stitch of D. Knit 8 rows. Bind off, leaving

last stitch on needle and do not break yarn. Turn work clockwise, pick up and knit 19 more stitches from next edge—20 stitches. Knit 8 rows. Bind off and break yarn.

FINISHING

Arrange 4 Squares each for Front and Back of Purse and sew together.

SIDE—MAKE 2

With B, cast on 7 stitches. Knit 80 rows. Bind off.

BASE

With A, cast on 7 stitches. Knit 80 rows. Bind off.

Sew 3 Side seams, leaving 4th seam unsewn for now. Sew Base to lower edge of Front only. Entire Purse should still lay flat for easy lining. With right side facing and C, pick up and knit 92 stitches across top edge of Purse. Knit 1 row. Bind off. Weave in ends.

Trace around flat Purse piece onto paper side of fusible adhesive. Use ruler to straighten lines and corners. Fuse fusible adhesive to wrong side of lining fabric following product instructions. Cut out through all layers along traced lines. Peel off paper backing. Turn lining over, adhesive side down, onto wrong side of knit Purse. Fuse to knitting using low heat and firm pressure. Do not slide iron while fusing. Make sure lining piece matches knit edges all around.

Now sew remaining Side seam and remaining 3 seams around Purse Base.

HANDLE

With D, cast on 7 stitches. Knit every row to desired length. Bind off. Cut fusible adhesive and lining fabric to same width as handle and 2" (5 cm) longer. Fuse fusible adhesive to wrong side of lining fabric. Trim ½" (13 mm) off width, then turn over and fuse to wrong side of knit Handle, leaving 1" (2.5 cm) overhang at each end.

Sew Handle to top edge of Purse at sides. Fuse lining overhang to inside of Purse.

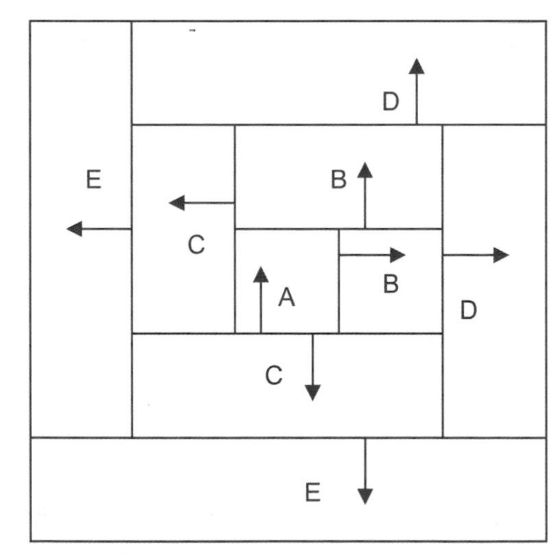

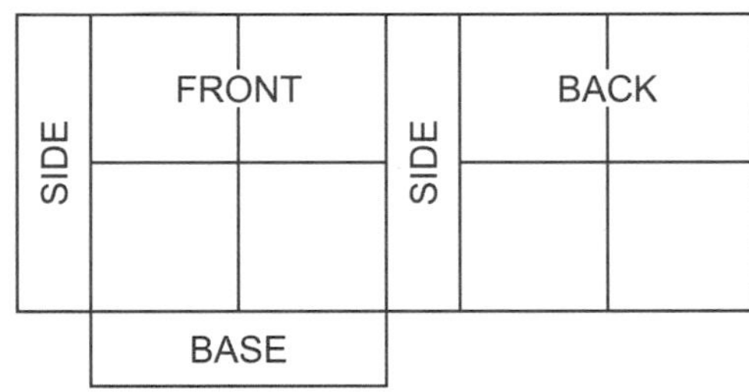

Assembly Diagram

AUTUMN STRIPES BAG

DESIGNED BY VLADIMIR TERIOKHIN

CROCHET/EASY

Crocheting ribbon yarn at a tighter gauge strengthens the resulting fabric. Stand-out details include subtle textured stripes and contrasting velvety soft handles.

SIZE

12" wide x 10" tall (30.5 x 25.5 cm), excluding Handle

MATERIALS

LION BRAND INCREDIBLE
100% POLYMIDE 1¾ OZ (50 G)
110 YD (100 M) SKEIN

5 balls #206 Autumn Leaves (MC) or color of your choice

LION BRAND LION SUEDE
100% POLYESTER 3 OZS (85 G)
122 YARDS (110 M) BALL

1 ball #126 Coffee (CC) or color of your choice

- Size G-6 (4 mm) crochet hook *or size to obtain gauge*
- Sewing needle and matching thread
- Large-eyed, blunt needle

GAUGE

16 double crochet = 4" (10 cm) with MC; 7 rows = 3" (7.5 cm) in double crochet with MC.
Be sure to check your gauge.

STITCH EXPLANATIONS

Shell (3 double crochet, chain 1, 3 double crochet) in same stitch.

dc2tog (double crochet decrease) Yarn over, insert hook into stitch and draw up a loop, yarn over and draw through 2 loops. Yarn over, insert hook in next stitch and draw up a loop. Yarn over, draw through 2 loops; yarn over, draw through all loops on hook.

3dc–Cluster [Yarn over, insert hook in next stitch and draw up a loop, yarn over and draw through 2 loops] 3 times; yarn over, draw through all loops on hook.

4dc–Cluster [Yarn over, insert hook in next stitch and draw up a loop, yarn over and draw through 2 loops] 4 times; yarn over, draw through all loops on hook.

7dc–Cluster [Yarn over, insert hook in next stitch and draw up a loop, yarn over and draw through 2 loops] 7 times; yarn over, draw through all loops on hook.

PATTERN STITCH

Reverse Sc *Insert hook in next stitch to the right, yarn over, draw yarn through stitch, yarn over, draw yarn through 2 loops on hook; repeat from * across.

NOTE

Bag is made of a Front, a Back, a Gusset for sides, and 2 Handles.

FRONT/BACK—MAKE 2

Starting at bottom edge, with MC, chain 45.

Row 1 Double crochet in 3rd chain from hook and in each chain across to last chain, 2 double crochet in last chain. Turn—45 stitches.

Rows 2–6 Chain 3, double crochet in first double crochet, double crochet in each double crochet across to last double crochet, 2 double crochet in last double crochet. Turn—55 double crochet at end of Row 6.

Row 7 Chain 1, single crochet in first stitch, *skip next 2 stitches, shell in next stitch, skip next 2 stitches, single crochet in next stitch; repeat from * across. Turn—9 shells.

Row 8 Chain 3, 3dc-cluster in next 3 stitches, chain 2, single crochet in next chain 1-space, chain 2, *7dc-cluster in next 7 stitches, chain 2, single crochet in next chain 1-space, chain 2; repeat from * across to last 4 stitches, 4dc-cluster in last 4 stitches. Turn—8 7dc-clusters.

Row 9 Chain 3, 3 double crochet in first stitch, skip next chain 2-space, single crochet in next single crochet, skip next chain 2-space, *shell in next cluster, skip next chain 2-space, single crochet in next single crochet, skip next chain 2-space; repeat from * across to last cluster, 4 double crochet in last cluster. Turn—8 shells.

Row 10 Chain 1, single crochet in first double crochet, *chain 2, 7dc-cluster in next 7 stitches, chain 2, single crochet in next chain 1-space; repeat from * across, ending with single crochet in top of turning chain. Turn—9 7dc-clusters.

Rows 11–14 Repeat Rows 7–10.

Row 15 Chain 3, *2 double crochet in next chain 2-space, double crochet in next cluster, 2 double crochet in next chain 2-space, skip next single crochet; repeat from * across to last stitch, double crochet in last single crochet. Turn—47 dc.

Row 16 Chain 2, double crochet in each double crochet across to last 2 stitches, dc2tog in last 2 stitches. Turn—45 dc.

Rows 17–24 Chain 2, double crochet in each double crochet across to last 2 double crochet, dc2tog in last 2 dc. Turn, leaving turning chain unworked—29 double crochet at end of Row 24. Fasten off MC.

GUSSET

With MC, chain 8.

Row 1 Double crochet in 4th chain from hook and in each chain across. Turn—6 stitches.

Rows 2–61 Chain 3, double crochet in each stitch across. Turn. Fasten off MC.

HANDLE—MAKE 2

With CC, chain 5.

Row 1 Double crochet in 3rd chain from hook, double crochet in last chain. Turn—3 stitches.

Rows 2–48 Chain 3, double crochet in each stitch across. Turn. Fasten off CC.

FINISHING

With wrong side facing, using large-eyed, blunt needle and MC, sew Gusset around 3 sides of Front. Sew opposite side of Gusset around 3 sides of Back to correspond.

TOP EDGING

Round 1 With right side of Bag facing, join MC at one seam on top edge, chain 1, working from left to right, reverse second crochet in each stitch around. Join with slip stitch in first reverse second crochet. Fasten off MC.

HANDLE ASSEMBLY

Weave one end of one Handle vertically through the stitches of the Front approximately 2" (5 cm) in from side edge, working in and out of the fabric 5 times, evenly spaced across from top to bottom as pictured. Repeat on opposite side of front with other end of same Handle, in corresponding position. Attach other Handle on back in same manner, making sure Handles are even above top edge of Bag. With sewing needle and thread, sew each Handle to top edge of Bag. Sew bottom ends of each Handle to inside of Bag to secure.

4.

EVENING KNOCKOUTS

Fashion glitzy yarn into evening bags with stunning textures in both knit and crochet. Shiny, sparkling yarn is strung with dazzling glass beads to catch the light on a vintage-inspired bag. Fun Fur and feathers plump up a handbag that is sophisticated and charming. The crocheted version of the same bag uses a fur yarn with additional texture for a standout look. A metallic gold clutch is compact yet roomy enough for everything you need for a night on the town.

VENUS CLUTCH

DESIGNED BY CATHY MAGUIRE

CROCHET/EASY

Transform a crocheted doily into a sophisticated evening bag by adding a reinforced lining and zipper.

SIZE

10½" wide x 5½" tall (26.5 x 14 cm)

MATERIALS

LION BRAND LAMÉ
65% RAYON, 35% METALIZED POLYESTER 75 YARDS (67 M)

2 spools #170 Gold or color of your choice

- Size C-2 (2.75 mm) crochet hook *or size to obtain gauge*
- Two 8" x 12" (20.5 x 30.5 cm) antique white felt panels
- One sheet 10-gauge mesh plastic canvas
- One 14" (35.5 cm) nylon all-purpose zipper in Natural
- One beaded tassel
- Sewing needle
- Cream-colored machine sewing thread
- Large-eyed, blunt needle

GAUGE

26 single crochet + 30 rows = 4" (10 cm).
Be sure to check your gauge.

STITCH EXPLANATION

Shell 5 double crochet in same stitch.

FRONT

Chain 5. Join with slip stitch to form ring.
Round 1 (right side) Chain 2, work 19 double crochet in ring. Join with slip stitch in top of beginning chain. Turn—20 stitches.
Round 2 (wrong side) Chain 2, *2 double crochet in next double crochet, double crochet in next double crochet; repeat from * around, ending with 2 double crochet in last stitch. Join with slip stitch in top of beginning chain. Turn—30 stitches.
Round 3 Chain 2, double crochet in same stitch, * double crochet in each of next 2 double crochet, 2 double crochet in next double crochet; repeat from * around, ending with double crochet in last chain. Join with slip stitch in top of beginning chain. Turn—40 stitches.
Round 4 Chain 3, (double crochet, chain 1) in each double crochet around. Join with slip stitch in 2nd chain of beginning chain. Turn—40 chain 1-spaces.
Round 5 Chain 3, skip first chain 1-space, [double crochet, chain 1] in each chain 1-space around. Join with slip stitch in 2nd chain of beginning chain. Turn.
Rounds 6–9 Chain 2, double crochet in first chain 1-space, chain 1, [2 double crochet, chain 1] in each chain 1-space around. Join with slip

stitch in top of beginning chain. Turn.

Rounds 10–11 Chain 2, 2 double crochet in first chain 1-space, chain 1, [3 double crochet, chain 1] in each chain 1-space around. Join with slip stitch in top of beginning chain. Turn.

Round 12 Chain 2, 2 double crochet in first chain 1-space, chain 1, *[3 double crochet, chain 1, 3 double crochet, chain 1] in next chain 1-space, [3 double crochet, chain 1] in next chain 1-space; repeat from * around, ending with [3 double crochet, chain 1, 3 double crochet, chain 1] in last chain 1-space. Join with slip stitch in top of beginning chain. Turn—60 chain 1-spaces.

Rounds 13–16 Repeat Round 10.

Round 17 Chain 1, single crochet in each stitch and space around. Join with slip stitch in first single crochet. Turn—240 single crochet.

Round 18 Chain 1, *single crochet in single crochet, skip next single crochet, shell in next single crochet, skip next single crochet; repeat from * around. Join with slip stitch in first single crochet. Turn—60 shells.

Round 19 Chain 2, 2 double crochet in first single crochet, skip next 2 double crochet, single crochet in next double crochet, skip next 2 double crochet, *shell in next single crochet, skip next 2 double crochet, single crochet in next double crochet, skip next 2 double crochet; repeat from * around, ending with 2 double crochet in first single crochet already holding 3 stitches. Join with slip stitch in top of beginning chain. Turn—60 shells. Fasten off.

FINISHING

Cut out the lining pattern twice using the felt pieces. (The lining Front, Back, and Bottom are cut in one piece.) Sandwich 2 linings and machine- or hand-sew the 2 layers together along sewing lines in the center of the lining.

Cut an 8½" x ¾" (21.5 x 2 cm) piece of plastic canvas and an 8" (20.5 cm) circle of plastic canvas. Cut the circle in half.

Slide the rectangle of plastic canvas between the 2 layers of lining. Place the 2 semi circles between the 2 layers of lining on the front and back and secure with a line of machine- or hand-sewing all the way around the circle.

Fold the 1" (2.5 cm) zipper allowance (pull end) to the inside and place the zipper at the bottom of the Bag lining, wrong side to wrong side. Pin one edge of the zipper to the round edge of the Bag Front. Pin the other zipper edge to the edge of the Bag Back. Slip stitch both seams and fold the excess zipper (at the end) to the inside of the Bag.

Slip stitch along the bottom at the side of the Bag. Place crocheted panel over the finished lining with the ruffled edge overlapping the zipper and lining edge. Slip stitch or tack crocheted panel to lining with a small running stitch. Sew the beaded tassel (to be used as a decorative zipper pull) to the zipper with several stitches using sewing needle and sewing thread.

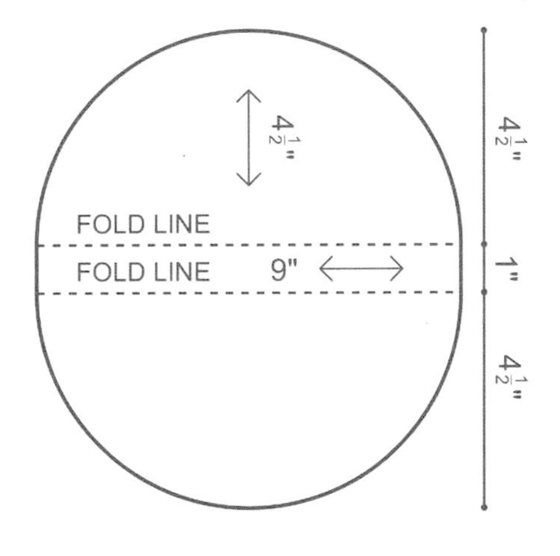

DIETRICH DRAWSTRING

DESIGNED BY CATHY MAGUIRE

KNIT/EASY

The glass beads and sparkly yarn are perfect partners for this 1930s-inspired evening bag. The prestrung beads are knit in columns between garter stitch ribs.

SIZE

Base 4" (10 cm) diameter
Height 7" (18 cm), excluding Drawstring

MATERIALS

LION BRAND GLITTERSPUN
60% ACRYLIC, 13% POLYESTER, 27% CUPRO
1¾ OZ (50G) 115 YD BALL

1 ball #135 Bronze or color of your choice

- Size 8 (5 mm) 16" (40.5 cm) circular needle *or size to obtain gauge*
- Small amount of strong thread for stringing beads
- Darning needle (must fit through beads)
- Beeswax
- One 3 oz (100 g)package Jewelry & Craft Essentials Glass Rochaille "E" beads (size 6/0)
- One plastic canvas 4" (10 cm) round (7 mesh)
- Size 16 tapestry needle
- Stitch markers

GAUGE

18 stitches + 26 rounds = 4" (10 cm) in garter stitch (Knit 1 round, purl 1 round).
Be sure to check your gauge.

STRING BEADS

Fold 12" (30.5 cm) of strong thread in half and thread it through the darning needle. Thread yarn through the thread loop and pull 1–2" (2.5–5 cm) through. Apply beeswax to the yarn end to make the beads slide on a little more easily. You may need to thread your needle a couple of times to string all the beads.
Before casting on, string 816 beads onto yarn. For the first 10 rows of beading, 4 beads will be strung and knit 8 times a row (320 beads total). For the second 10 rows of beading, 3 beads will be strung and knit 8 times a row (240 beads). For the third 10 rows of beading, 2 beads will be strung and knit 8 times a row (160 beads). For the last 12 rows of beading, 1 bead will be strung and knit 8 times a row (96 beads).

BAG

Cast on 64 stitches. Place marker and join for working in the round, being careful not to twist.
Rounds 1–6 Work in garter stitch, beginning with a purl round.
Round 7 *Bind off 3 stitches (1 stitch on needle), purl 4; repeat from * around—40 stitches.
Rounds 8–17 *Slide 4 beads to needle, work 5 stitches in garter stitch; repeat from * around.

Rounds 18–27 *Slide 3 beads to needle, work 5 stitches in garter stitch; repeat from * around.
Rounds 28–37 *Slide 2 beads to needle, work 5 stitches in garter stitch; repeat from * around.
Rounds 38–49 *Slide 1 bead to needle, work 5 stitches in garter stitch; repeat from * around.
Rounds 50–51 Work in garter stitch.
Round 52 *Bind off 1 stitch (1 stitch on needle), knit 18; repeat from * once more.
Round 53 Purl, casting on 1 stitch over each bound off stitch in previous row.
Rounds 54–55 Work in garter stitch. Bind off all stitches. Cut yarn, leaving a 24" (61 cm) tail to sew casing.

FINISHING

Fold bound-off edge to inside of Bag, just above last row of beaded knitting. Whipstitch bound-off edge to Bag to form casing, making sure stitches don't show on right side.

DRAWSTRING—MAKE 2

Cut 3 strands of yarn, each 30" (76 cm) long. Tie ends together with a single knot about 4" (10 cm) from the ends. Braid 3 yarn ends together and finish with a single knot 4" (10 cm) from the bottom.

Using a small safety pin, thread 1 drawstring through one of the holes in the casing at the top of the bag. Pull through casing and out the same hole. Join the 2 ends together with a single knot under the 4" (10 cm) knots. Thread the other drawstring in the same way through the other hole in the casing and finish in the same way. Pull both drawstrings tightly.

BASE

Thread the size 16 tapestry needle with a long length of yarn. Cover the 4" (10 cm) plastic canvas round with a combination of slip stitches and back stitches. Choose a right side. When you run out of yarn, pull the yarn end to the wrong side, start a new yarn end, and knot the 2 ends together. You will have at least 7 knotted ends by the time you fill the round. Make enough back and slip stitches to cover the plastic canvas on the right side. Trim all ends.
Pin bottom edge of Bag evenly around Base and whipstitch together. Weave in ends.

ALL ABOUT EVENING KNIT BAG

DESIGNED BY

CATHY MAGUIRE

KNIT/EASY

Sized for an evening's essentials, this chic bag is disarmingly soft. The full lining, reinforced handles, and snap closure make it as practical as it is fashionable. Stitch one up in knit, as here, or crochet, as on pages 62–63.

SIZE

9½ " wide x 6" long (24 x 15 cm), excluding Handle

MATERIALS

LION BRAND FUN FUR
100% POLYESTER 1¾ OZ
(50 G) 64 YD (58 M) BALL

1 ball #098 Ivory (A)
1 ball #124 Champagne (B)
1 ball #205 Sandstone (C)
or colors of your choice

- Size 10 (6 mm) knitting needles *or size to obtain gauge*

- Sewing needle and thread to match yarn
- 1 sheet mesh plastic canvas in gauge 10
- 1 pack ZFR Feathers B163 Hackle Red
- 1 pack Aqua Culture standard airline tubing (25" [23 m])
- 1 hank perle cotton size 8, in ivory (DMC #838)
- ½" (13 mm) magnet purse snap
- ½ yd (0.5 m) ivory colored felt
- Large-eyed, blunt needle

GAUGE

11 stitches + 13 rows = 4" (10 cm) in garter stitch (knit every row).
Be sure to check your gauge.

STITCH EXPLANATIONS

M1 (make 1 stitch) An increase worked by lifting the horizontal thread lying between the needles and placing it onto the left needle. Work this new stitch through the back loop.
skp Slip 1 as if to knit, knit 1, pass slipped stitch over knit stitch.

NOTE

Bag is knit in 2 pieces with 1 strand each of A, B, and C held together. Bag lining is cut from purchased felt. The top of the Bag lining folds out to catch the top of the knitted panels and to encase the tops of the feathers.

BAG PANEL—MAKE 2

With 1 strand each of A, B, and C held together, cast on 22 stitches.
Row 1 and all odd-numbered rows Knit.
Rows 2 and 4 (Increase Row) Knit 1, M1, knit to last stitch, M1, knit 1.
Row 6 Knit.
Rows 8, 12, and 16 (Decrease Row) Knit 1, knit 2 together, knit to last 2 stitches, skp, knit 1.
Rows 10 and 14 Knit.
Bind off.

FINISHING

Cut 2 pieces of plastic canvas 7½" x 1" (19 x 2.5 cm). Cut 2 felt panels as shown in lining pattern. Press felt along 2 fold lines to form panels. Attach snap to felt panels and fold panels around plastic canvas. Set aside. Separate the feathers and place on right side of knitted pieces at top edge of Bag and stitch securely. Pin the pressed lining opening across the feathers and knitted panels and, with perle cotton, sew a ⅛" (3 mm) running stitch across the front of each panel (encasing tops of feathers). Sew side seams of linings together. Sew knitted panels together. Weave in ends.

HANDLE

Cut a 17½" (44.5 cm) length of tubing. Cut a 1" x 17½" (2.5 x 44.5 cm) piece of felt. Wrap felt around tubing and, with perle cotton, blanket stitch along length. Place Handle inside top of Bag with blanket stitches facing inward. Sew Handle in place with perle cotton, going through all layers.

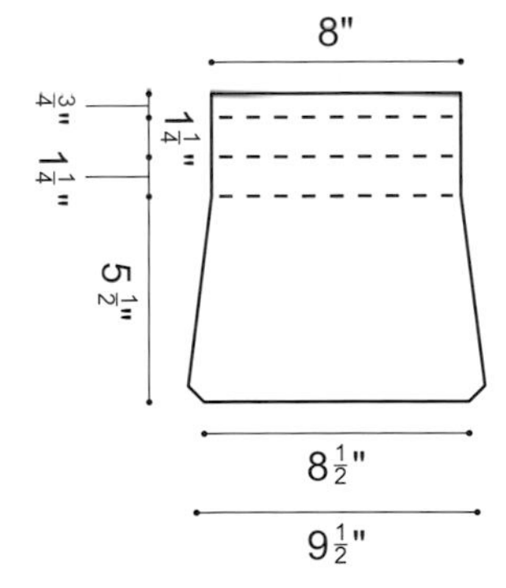

ALL ABOUT EVENING CROCHET BAG

DESIGNED BY CATHY MAGUIRE

KNIT/EASY

Like its knit cousin (see page 60), this soft yet sturdy knockout will take you through the evening in style.

SIZE

10" wide x 7" tall (25.5 x 18 cm), plus Handle

MATERIALS

LION BRAND FANCY FUR
55% POLYAMIDE, 45% POLYESTER
1¾ OZ (50G) 39 YD (35.5 M) BALL

2 balls #255 Jungle Print or color of your choice

- Size N-13 (9 mm) crochet hook *or size to obtain gauge*
- 1 yd (0.9 m) black ultrasuede fabric or wool felt
- One skein DMC perle cotton, #310 Black
- Size 26 tapestry needle or large-eyed needle for perle cotton
- One ½" (13 mm) Sewing Basket magnetic purse snap
- One pack (25" [23 m]) Aqua Culture standard airline tubing

GAUGE

7 single crochet + 8 rows = 4" (10 cm).

Be sure to check your gauge.

STITCH EXPLANATION

sc2tog (single crochet decrease)
Insert hook into stitch and draw up a loop. Insert hook into next stitch and draw up a loop. Yarn over, draw through all 3 loops on hook.

FRONT/BACK—MAKE 2

Chain 17.

Row 1 (Right Side) Single crochet in 2nd chain from hook and in each chain across. Turn—16 single crochet.

Row 2 Chain 1, 2 single crochet in first single crochet, single crochet in each single crochet across to last single crochet, 2 single crochet in last single crochet. Turn—18 single crochet.

Rows 3–4 Chain 1, single crochet in each single crochet across. Turn.

Rows 5–10 Repeat Rows 2–4—total of 22 single crochet at end of Row 10.

Row 11 Chain 1, single crochet 2 together in first 2 stitches, single crochet in each stitch across to last 2 stitches, single crochet 2 together in last 2 stitches. Turn—20 single crochet.

Rows 12–14 Repeat Row 3.

Fasten off. Weave in ends.

ASSEMBLY

Following lining pattern (see page 60), cut 1 piece of ultrasuede fabric for each of Front and Back lining. The top of the lining folds out to catch the top of the crocheted panels and to encase the tops of the fur. Following the 2 fold lines, press the tops of the Bag linings in place. Attach magnet snap as indicated on lining pattern, facing inside. With tapestry needle and perle cotton, using a whipstitch or a running stitch, sew each lining piece to corresponding crocheted Front or Back along sewing lines indicated on pattern. Pin the pressed lining opening across the crocheted Front and Back top and sew a running stitch across the front of the Bag (encasing crocheted panels). The stitches should be ⅛" (3 mm) and the gaps between the stitches should be a little smaller. Start and finish with a double knot on the inside of Bag. Sew both lining pieces together with a running stitch. Sew both crocheted panels together.

HANDLE

Cut a 1" x 16" (2.5 x 40.5 cm) piece of ultrasuede and a 15" (38 cm) length of tubing. Wrap the ultrasuede around the tubing and sew in place with a row of running stitches followed by a row of blanket stitches. Place the ends of the Handle inside the top of the Bag, lining up the round part of the Handle to the edge of the Bag, with the blanket stitch edge on the inside. Slip stitch both Handle ends into place. On the outside, with a running stitch, join the front and back of Bag, stitching through the Handle ends to help secure them in place. Start and finish with a double back stitch and a single knot.

5.

FORM FOLLOWS FUNCTION

The bags in this chapter are designed to make life easier for people on the go. The Yoga Bag holds your rolled mat neatly, and features a comfortable shoulder strap attached by swivel snaphooks, making navigating subways and buses a breeze. The Knit and Go Tote has a built-in tool belt for ready access to all your odds and ends. The Graduate bag is as beautiful as it is practical. The Messenger Bag offers a great chance to stitch up something useful while fueling your creativity with color and texture—its reinforced interior is surprisingly spacious, allowing plenty of room for school supplies, books, or just about anything.

KNIT AND GO TOTE

DESIGNED BY CATHY MAGUIRE

KNIT/EASY

Featuring ribbon pockets for all your needles and tools, this bag is reinforced with nylon webbing and generously sized to carry everything you'll need for multiple projects.

SIZE

16" wide x 16" long x 5" deep (40.5 x 40.5 x 12.5 cm), excluding Handles

MATERIALS

LION BRAND LANDSCAPES
50% WOOL, 50% ACRYLIC
1¾ OZ (50G) 55 YD (50 M) BALL

7 balls #273 Spring Desert or color of your choice

- Size 11 (8 mm) knitting needles *or size to obtain gauge*
- 2 sheets 8" x 12" (20.5 x 30.5 cm) mesh plastic canvas (10 gauge)
- 4½ yd (4.5 m) 1" (25 cm) nylon webbing
- 8 yd (7 m) 1⅜" (35 cm) polyester wired ribbon
- #16 size blunt-eyed yarn needle
- Sewing thread to match webbing
- 4 oz (113g) Fabri-Tac permanent adhesive

GAUGE

10 stitches + 15 rows = 4" (10 cm) in stockinette stitch (knit on right side, purl on wrong side).
Be sure to check your gauge.

NOTE

When using Lion Brand Landscapes to sew seams, twist the yarn to maintain its strength.

BASE—MAKE 2

Cast on 13 stitches. Work 60 rows in stockinette stitch. Bind off all stitches. Break yarn, leaving a 30" (76 cm) tail for sewing.

FRONT

Cast on 52 stitches. Work 60 rows in stockinette stitch. Bind off all stitches.

BACK

Work as for Front.

PLASTIC CANVAS BASE

Cut 3 pieces, each 5" x 13½" (12.5 x 34.5 cm), of plastic canvas and set 2 aside. From 3rd piece, cut 2 pieces 5" x 2½" (12.5 x 6.5 cm) and 2 pieces 5" x 1" (12.5 x 2.5 cm). (These 4 pieces will be used to extend the pieces set aside.)
Place one 5" x 13½" (12.5 x 34.5 cm) piece next to one 5" x 2½" (12.5 x 6.5 cm) piece. Place a 5" x 1" (12.5 x 2.5 cm) piece over the join to stop the join from bending. Whipstitch the 2 layers together using buttonhole thread. Repeat for the 2nd Base.
Lay one 5" x 16" (12.5 x 40.5 cm) Base over the other with the joins on opposite ends. Sew together at the corners.

FINISHING

BAG

Sew Front to Back with an invisible seam along both side seams. Weave in ends.

BASE

Sandwich the plastic canvas Base between the 2 knit Base pieces with right sides facing out. Whipstitch around edges using the 30" (76 cm) tail. Weave in ends.

NYLON WEBBING

Cut 2 lengths, each 16½" (42 cm) for topstitching over side seams; 2 lengths 43" (109 cm) (one for top edge of Bag and one for Tool Belt base); and 2 lengths 15" (38 cm) for Handles. Apply a small amount of adhesive to cut edges to prevent raveling.

Sew the ends together on each 43" (109 cm) length with ½" (13 mm) seam allowance to form 2 closed loops.

Pin the 16½" (42 cm) lengths to side seams so that there is ½" (13 mm) extra on the bottom. Secure using buttonhole thread with running stitch spaced ¼" (6 mm) apart.

Pin one piece of the 43" (109 cm) webbings around the top, easing to fit, and allowing the bound-off edge to show. Mark the 4 corners with pins. Center the Handles under the webbing on Front and Back 3" (7.5 cm) from corners. Sew around top edge to secure.

Cut 2 lengths 5" x ¾" (12.5 cm x 19 mm) from plastic canvas left-overs. Insert under the webbing at the sides of the Bag. Sew across the lower edge of the webbing to encase. Sew 4 vertical lines across the webbing to secure.

Whipstitch Base to the Bag on all 4 sides, matching corners with marks. Weave in ends.

TOOL BELT

Cut 3 lengths 29" (74 cm) of ribbon for large needles; 3 lengths 26" (66 cm) for medium needles; 2 lengths 23" (58.5 cm) for small needles; 2 lengths 19" (48.5 cm) for double-pointed needles; and 2 lengths 10" (25.5 cm) for needle holders, tape measure, or small scissors. Make a double ¼" (6 mm) fold to finish the top and bottom of the ribbons. Fold ribbons in half (wrong sides together). Sew side seams on ribbons to form individual pockets.

Mark the 4 corners on the second 43" (109 cm) webbing. Pin the first long ribbon pocket on the long side of the webbing 1" (2.5 cm) from the first corner, and pin the next 5 ribbons 1" (2.5 cm) apart. The tops of the pockets should line up with the top of the webbing. Apply the other 6 ribbon pockets to the other long side of the webbing, starting with the longest pocket and working down to the smallest ones. Sew all the pockets to the webbing with a couple of backstitches to both sides of pocket at the top of the webbing. Pin the Tool Belt inside the Bag 3" (7.5 cm) from the top and match all corners. Take care not to distort the direction of the knitting by pinning the webbing to the Bag between each ribbon pocket; check the Bag from the outside before you sew. Secure the Belt to the Bag with a few backstitches on the webbing between pockets and across the 5" (12.5 cm) of webbing at both sides.

YOGA BAG

DESIGNED BY CATHY MAGUIRE

KNIT/EASY

Take a break from stitching and go for a stretch! This simple bag carries your yoga mat in style. The easy-to-find hardware and nylon webbing straps make the bag perfectly practical.

SIZE

Fits a standard yoga mat 24" x 68" (61 x 172.5 cm), rolled tightly
Approximately 24" (61 cm) wide (slightly stretched) x 4" (10 cm) in diameter, excluding Shoulder Strap

MATERIALS

LION BRAND WOOL-EASE THICK & QUICK 80% ACRYLIC 20% WOOL 6 OZ (170 G) 108 YD (97 M) BALL

2 balls #149 Charcoal or color of your choice

- Size 13 (9 mm) knitting needles *or size to obtain gauge*
- Two 4" (10 cm) rounds Quick Shape Plastic Canvas (7 mesh)
- 2 yards (2 m) 1" (2.5 cm) red nylon webbing
- 2 Buckleworks black plastic swivel snaphooks
- 2 Buckleworks black plastic center release buckles
- Two 1" (2.5 cm) wide D-rings
- Size 16 yarn needle
- Sewing needle and red thread

GAUGE

9 stitches + 12 rows = 4" (10 cm) in stockinette stitch (knit on right side, purl on wrong side).
Be sure to check your gauge.

PATTERN STITCH

Seed Stitch (odd number of stitches)
Row 1 *Knit 1, purl 1; repeat from *, ending knit 1.
Repeat Row 1 for seed stitch.

KNIT PANEL

Cast on 47 stitches. Work 4 rows in seed stitch.
Rows 5–42 Work 3 stitches in seed stitch, work in stockinette stitch to last 3 stitches, work 3 stitches in seed stitch.
Work 4 rows in seed stitch. Bind off all stitches.

PLASTIC CANVAS ROUNDS

Make a large center hole in each plastic canvas round by cutting the center cross (4 holes) carefully with small scissors or a craft knife. Thread the needle with a long length of yarn and start to wrap yarn around the plastic canvas.
Note You will need a few lengths of yarn to wrap the whole round. Weave in the end before starting a new strand. Use pliers to help pull the needle through if you have difficulty toward the end.
First, wrap the inner half of the circle by coming up through the center hole and sewing into the 6th row of holes from the center, skipping every other hole. Pull yarn

tightly after each wrap.
Now wrap the outer half of the circle by coming up through the first missed hole of the 6th row and into the last row of holes. Since there are 46 holes in the 6th row and 88 holes in the last row, you will need to use most of the holes in the 6th row twice.
Weave in ends.

SHOULDER STRAP AND CLOSURES

Cut 1 yard (1 m) of webbing for the shoulder strap and thread each end into a swivel snaphook. Fold ½" (13 mm) of webbing under twice and secure swivel snaphook with 2 rows of backstitching, starting and finishing with 2 double stitches.
Cut two 2" (5 cm) pieces of webbing and thread through the D-rings. Sew the 2 ends together as above.
Cut two 16" (40.5 cm) pieces of webbing and thread each end through the 2 parts of the center release buckles. Fold ¼" (6 mm) of webbing under twice and secure to both ends of the center release buckles. Sew webbing securely to all buckle parts as above.

ASSEMBLY

Sew the webbing pieces with the D-rings to the top of the Plastic Canvas Rounds. Pin side edges of the Knit Panel to the rounds, overlapping the seed stitch borders and easing the extra fabric around. Whipstitch in place using sewing thread. Pin straps 6½" (16.5 cm) from the ends and sew securely using sewing thread. Clip Shoulder Strap onto D-rings.

THE GRADUATE

DESIGNED BY MARIE HONAN

CROCHET/INTERMEDIATE

This beautiful bag is created by crocheting a solid-color yarn around a multicolor strand. Plastic canvas gives structure to the bag and makes it strong enough for all your books and binders.

SIZE

14" wide x 12" tall (35.5 x 30.5 cm), excluding Strap

MATERIALS

LION BRAND WOOL-EASE
80% ACRYLIC, 20% WOOL
3 OZ (85 G) 179 YD (180 M) BALL

3 balls #177 Loden (A) or color of your choice

LION BRAND LANDSCAPES
50% WOOL, 50% ACRYLIC
1¾ OZ (50 G) 55 YARD (50 M)

4 balls #273 Spring Desert (B) or color of your choice

- Size J-10 (6 mm) crochet hook *or size to obtain gauge*
- One sheet 10 gauge plastic mesh canvas
- Two ½" (13 mm) magnetic purse snaps
- Large-eyed, blunt needle

GAUGE

(Single crochet, chain 1) 9 times + 12 rows = 4" (10 cm) in Woven Crochet pattern.
Be sure to check your gauge.

PATTERN STITCH

Woven Crochet

Row 1 Holding 1 strand of A and 2 strands of B together, make an overhand knot at the end. Keep A to the back and top and B to the front and bottom. A is the working thread and B is held with the thumb and index finger of both left and right hands to keep it secure, straight, and at an even tension. Yarn over with A, pull to the front, and make a chain so that it is on top of B. Insert hook under B, *yarn over with A and pull to the front, yarn over, draw yarn through 2 loops on hook (single crochet made), chain 1; repeat from * for desired length of row, single crochet over B strand. Turn. **Note** In this stitch, pieces are not begun with a set number of chains, but are worked for the number of inches (cm) given for each section.

Row 2 Chain 1, keeping B to the front and A to the back, *single crochet in next single crochet of previous row, chain 1; repeat from * across, single crochet in last single crochet. Turn.

Repeat Row 2 until piece is desired length.

NOTE

Consistent tension is important. Make sure that your single crochet stitches in A are loose enough so that they don't squash B strands. Use a larger crochet hook if you find the crochet too tight. Keep the crochet tight enough to have a stable fabric. The chain stitches allow

B to show through, so keep them very consistent. Practice with some swatches until you achieve a satisfactory tension. The fabric has a lot of stretch widthwise and is stable lengthwise.

BODY

Note Body is worked in one piece in vertical rows of woven crochet.

Row 1 Work in woven crochet until Row 1 measures 38" (96.5 cm) from beginning. Turn.

Row 2 Work Row 2 of woven crochet pattern.

Repeat Row 2 until Body measures 14" (35.5 cm) from beginning. Fasten off.

STRAP

Row 1 Work in woven crochet until piece measures 76" (193 cm) from beginning. Turn.

Row 2 Work Row 2 of woven crochet pattern.

Repeat Row 2 until Strap measures 2¼" (5.5 cm) from beginning. Fasten off.

SIDE—MAKE 2

Row 1 Work in woven crochet until piece measures 11" (28 cm) from beginning. Turn.

Row 2 Work Row 2 of woven crochet pattern.

Repeat Row 2 until Side measures 2½" (6.5 cm) from beginning. Fasten off.

ASSEMBLY

For bottom of the Bag, cut a piece of plastic canvas 17 squares wide x 90 squares long—approximately 2¼" x 14" (5.5 x 35.5 cm). Position plastic canvas for bottom horizontally over inside of Body, 23½" (59.5 cm) from top edge and 12" (30.5 cm) from bottom edge. Sew plastic canvas to Body using large-eyed, blunt needle and A, working one stitch for every 10th square of canvas, and 4 squares in from the edge, making sure that stitches don't cover B strands on Body. Without twisting Strap, lay ends of Strap over plastic canvas bottom, with 4" (10 cm) of Straps overlapping at center. With A, sew strap edges to bottom of Body on outside of plastic canvas bottom. For the Sides of the Bag, cut 2 pieces of plastic canvas 17 squares x 67 squares—approximately 2¼" x 10½" (5.5 x 26.5 cm). Place plastic canvas sides on inside of Straps, starting flush with bottom. Sew Strap to plastic canvas sides with A through each square on outer edge of plastic canvas. Place woven crochet Sides over plastic canvas sides on inside of Bag, with ½" (13 mm) excess folded over top of plastic canvas. Sew woven crochet Sides onto the plastic canvas, through the Strap on the bottom edge, and up the other side. At top edge, sew through folded edge of Side, the plastic canvas, and the Strap. Repeat on the other side. Sew over any exposed edges of plastic canvas. With A, sew side edges of Strap to Sides of Body using edge-to-edge seam. Attach magnet snaps approximately 2" (5 cm) from bottom and Sides of Bag.

MESSENGER BAG

DESIGNED BY DORIS CHAN

CROCHET/INTERMEDIATE

A classic shape is reinterpreted with a fresh palette and richly textured yarn.

SIZE

10¼" wide x 7¼" high x 1¼" deep (26 x 18.5 x 3 cm)
Handle 24" (61 cm) long (adjustable)

MATERIALS

LION BRAND LION SUEDE 100% POLYESTER 3 OZS (85 G) 122 YARDS (110 M) BALL

2 balls #113 Scarlet (A)
1 ball #098 Ecru (B)
1 ball #178 Teal (C)
or colors of your choice

- Size J-10 (6 mm) crochet hook *or size to obtain gauge*
- Scraps of contrasting yarn to be used as markers
- Large-eyed, blunt needle

GAUGE

12 single crochet + 14 rows = 4" (10 cm).

Be sure to check your gauge.

STITCH EXPLANATION

sc2tog (single crochet decrease)

Insert hook into stitch and draw up a loop. Insert hook into next stitch and draw up a loop. Yarn over, draw through all 3 loops on hook.

FRONT STRAP

Row 1 (Right Side) With A, chain 7, slip stitch in 7th chain from hook (loop), chain 20, single crochet in 2nd chain from hook and in each of next 18 chain, single crochet in next 3 chains of loop, 3 single crochet in next chain of loop, single crochet in next 3 chains of loop; working across opposite side of foundation chain, single crochet in each of 19 chain. Turn—47 single crochet.

Row 2 (Wrong Side) Chain 1, single crochet in first 22 single crochet, 2 single crochet in each of next 3 single crochet, single crochet in last 22 single crochet—50 single crochet. Fasten off A.

Row 3 (Right Side) With right side facing, join B in first single crochet, chain 1, single crochet in first 23 single crochet, 2 single crochet in next single crochet, single crochet in next 2 single crochet, 2 single crochet in next single crochet, single crochet in last 23 single crochet—52 single crochet. Fasten off B.

Row 4 (Wrong Side) With wrong side facing, join C in first single crochet, chain 1, single crochet in first single crochet, [chain 1, skip next single crochet, single crochet in next single crochet] 12 times, [chain 1, single crochet in next single crochet] 3 times, [chain 1, skip next single crochet, single crochet in next single crochet] 12 times—27 chain 1-spaces. Fasten off C. Weave in ends.

FRONT

Note This piece is a rectangle worked around a beginning chain, with 2 lower corners. Mark the middle single crochet of each corner and move markers up into the middle single crochet as you go.

With A, chain 8.

Row 1 (Right Side) Single crochet in 2nd chain from hook and in next 5 chain, 3 single crochet in last chain; working across opposite side of foundation chain, single crochet in each of next 6 chain. Turn—15 single crochet.

Row 2 Chain 1, single crochet in first 6 single crochet, 3 single crochet in next single crochet, place a marker in center single crochet for corner, single crochet in next single crochet, 3 single crochet in next single crochet, place a marker in center single crochet for corner, single crochet in last 6 single crochet. Turn—19 single crochet; 2 corners.

Row 3 Chain 1, single crochet in first 7 single crochet, 3 single crochet in corner single crochet, single crochet in next 3 single crochet, 3 single crochet in corner single crochet, single crochet in next 7 single crochet. Turn—23 single crochet.

Rows 4–17 Chain 1, [single crochet in each single crochet to next marked corner single crochet, 3 single crochet in corner single crochet] twice, single crochet in each single crochet across. Turn—79 single crochet at end of Row 17.

Row 18 (Wrong Side) Chain 1, single crochet in first 22 single crochet, 2 single crochet in corner single crochet, single crochet in next 33 single crochet, 2 single crochet in corner single crochet, single crochet in next 22 single crochet, drop corner markers, mark first and last single crochet of row—81 single crochet. Do not fasten off.

FRONT EDGING

Row 1 With wrong side facing, working across row-end stitches of Front, chain 1, single crochet in each row-end stitch across. Turn—36 single crochet.

Row 2 Slip stitch in each single crochet across—36 slip stitches. Fasten off. Weave in ends.

BACK

Work as for Front through Row 18. Fasten off.

FLAP

Row 1 (Right Side) With right side of Back facing, and row-end stitches positioned across top, skip first row-end single crochet, join A in next row-end single crochet, chain 1, single crochet in same row-end single crochet, single crochet in each of next 12 row-end stitches. Hold Front Strap in place at front of work, with wrong side facing; matching row-end stitches, working through double thickness, single crochet in each of next 8 row-end stitches; single crochet in each of next 13 row-end stitches of Back, leaving last row-end stitch unworked. Turn—34 single crochet.

Rows 2–15 Chain 1, single crochet in each single crochet across. Turn.

Rows 16–20 Chain 1, single crochet 2 together in first 2 stitches, single crochet in each single crochet to last 2 single crochet, single crochet 2 together in last 2 stitches. Turn—24 single crochet at end of Row 20. Fasten off.

FLAP EDGING

Row 1 With right side facing, join A in skipped (marked) single crochet of Row 18 on right side of Back, single crochet in first row-end stitch of Flap, single crochet in next 15 row-end stitches, 2 single crochet in next row-end stitch, single crochet in each of 3 remaining row-end stitches, single crochet in next 24 single crochet of Row 20, single crochet in next 3 row-end stitches, 2 single crochet in next row-end stitch, single crochet in remaining 16 row-end stitches, slip stitch in next skipped (marked) single crochet of Row 18 of Back. Turn—66 single crochet.

Row 2 Slip stitch in each single crochet across. Fasten off.
Weave in ends.

GUSSET AND HANDLE STRAP

Note Gusset and Handle Strap are worked in one piece around a long chain, with a loop on each end.
With A, chain 7, slip stitch in 7th chain from hook (loop), chain 168, slip stitch in 7th chain from hook (loop).

Round 1 (Wrong Side) Chain 1, single crochet in each of next 161 chains, *single crochet in each of next 3 chains of loop, 3 single crochet in next chain of loop, single crochet in remaining 3 chains of loop*; working across opposite side of foundation chain, single crochet in each of next 161 chains; repeat from * to * around other loop. Join with slip stitch in first single crochet. Turn—340 single crochet.

Round 2 (Right Side) Chain 1, *single crochet in first 3 single crochet of loop, 2 single crochet in each of next 3 single crochet, single crochet in next 3 single crochet of loop*, single crochet and mark next single crochet, single crochet in next 79 single crochet, single crochet and mark next single crochet, single crochet in next 80 single crochet; repeat from * to * around other loop, single crochet in next 80 single crochet, single crochet and mark next single crochet, single crochet in next 79 single crochet, single crochet and mark last single crochet. Join with slip stitch in first single crochet. Fasten off.

ASSEMBLY

ATTACH FRONT TO GUSSET BETWEEN MARKERS

Locate last single crochet worked (marked) on Gusset. With right sides of Front facing, hold Gusset in place behind Front, wrong sides together, matching markers and single crochet.

Row 1 (Right Side) Join B with slip stitch in marked single crochet, chain 1; working through double thickness, single crochet in marked single crochet, single crochet in each of next 79 single crochet, single crochet in last marked single crochet—81 single crochet. Fasten off B.

Row 2 (Wrong Side) With wrong side facing, join C in first single crochet, chain 1, single crochet in same single crochet, [chain 1, skip next single crochet, single crochet in next single crochet] 10 times; over corner work *chain 1, single crochet in next single crochet, chain 1, skip next single crochet, single crochet in next single crochet, chain 1, single crochet in next single crochet*, [chain 1, skip next single crochet, single crochet in next single crochet] 16 times along bottom; repeat from * to * for other corner, [chain 1, skip next single crochet, single crochet in next single crochet] 10 times. Fasten off.

Attach Back to Gusset

With right sides of Back facing, hold Gusset in place behind Back, wrong sides together, matching markers and single crochet. Attach as for Front, repeating Rows 1–2.

To make Handle, slip loop at free end of Strap through loop at Bag end, overlapping Strap to outside of Bag.

BUTTONS—MAKE 2 OR AS MANY AS DESIRED

With A, leaving a long tail, chain 2.

Round 1 (Right Side) 7 single crochet in 2nd chain from hook. Do not join. Work in a spiral, marking beginning of each Round, moving marker up as work progresses.

Round 2 2 single crochet in each single crochet around—14 single crochet.

Round 3 [Stitch 2 together in next 2 stitches] 7 times. Join with slip stitch in next single crochet. Fasten off, leaving a long tail.

Thread ending tail on large-eyed, blunt needle. With right side facing, weave tail through back loops of stitches of last Round; pull up gently to gather to back of Button. Pull beginning tail through center ring. Tie and knot beginning and ending tails together, flattening Button.

Using tails, sew Buttons to Bag. Sew 1 on Front, centered under loop of Front Strap. Adjust Handle Strap to desired length(s) by overlapping more or less. Sew Button(s) to outside of Strap at as many places as you would like adjustments.

6.

WE FELT LIKE KNITTING

Felting adds an entirely different feel to knits. The bags in this chapter all require felting, which tightens and shrinks knitted or crocheted fabric, making it firmer and stronger. To make felt, you need wool or yarns with a high percentage of wool, along with a bit of trial and error when it comes to swatching, washing, and steaming your project to the desired shape (see page 79 for detailed instructions). But have no fear: the Cut and Sew Bag offers a risk-free introduction to felting. Once you're comfortable with the process, check out the more intricate patterns for interesting and entertaining ideas!

FELTING TECHNIQUES

When knitting or crocheting something you want to felt, you should use a larger needle or hook than you normally would. Swatching is of the utmost importance. Make a large swatch (at least an 8" [20.5 cm] square) and felt it exactly as you plan to felt your finished project. If you plan on doing any kind of "knit in" or yarn finishes, include a sample in your swatch. The Pampered Puppy Bag (pages 90–93) has a double hem around the top edge of the bag. The swatch was finished with a double hem to see how two layers of knit would felt together. The Easter Basket (pages 86–87) includes felted fringe and ties. Any details like these should always be incorporated into your swatch.

There are three factors necessary for successful felting: water, temperature change, and agitation. Felting can be done by hand, but it is much faster and easier to use a washing machine. Use a long wash setting with hot water and a cold rinse. Use your regular detergent and add several sturdy items of clothing like jeans, clean canvas shoes, or tennis balls. Towels tend to embed lint into the felt so they should be avoided.

Regardless of the yarn you use, you may have to wash your project several times to felt it to your satisfaction. Felting is not an exact science. The water temperature, whether you have hard or soft water, the detergent, and the amount of agitation will all make a difference. The size of your project will also play a role. Large pieces felt differently than small pieces. To felt additionally, dry by machine on the regular setting until almost dry.

You can help your piece to fit the shape you want by manipulating it between washes. Steam lightly to the desired shape. The piece will still be quite pliable after the first few washes. Your final project should have stitches that are hard to distinguish.

Felting can be used for trims and handles too. The Felt-Trim Tote in chapter 7 has felted handles and webbing. The handles are felted around a core tube to make them sturdy and strong. The webbing is felted to fit the size of the bag with careful swatching and calculating. Felted webbing can be simplified by knitting lengths of webbing strips, felting them, and then cutting them to size. In other words felt, cut, and then sew. Felted fringe can also be made in strips. Knit or crochet a base strip (a few rows of knitting or crochet) and follow the fringing instructions for the Easter Basket (pages 86–87). If you do plan to make felted trim, make a few handles, fringes, and webbing strips at the same time and wash them all together.

Before felting

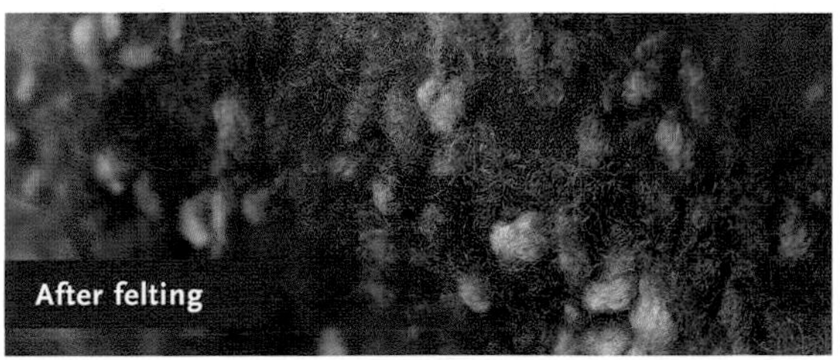
After felting

CUT AND SEW BAG

DESIGNED BY CATHY MAGUIRE

KNIT/EASY

This risk-free design gets you started on felting without having to worry about the variables. "Cut and sew" refers to the fashion industry practice of using knit yardage that is cut into pattern pieces and sewn together to make a garment. For this bag, you simply knit and felt two pieces, cut them to size, and sew them together. Since the pieces are felted before you cut, you don't need to worry about fraying.

SIZE

Bag 8" wide x 10" long (20.5 x 25.5 cm)
Strap 22" (56 cm)

MATERIALS

LION BRAND FISHERMEN'S WOOL 100% PURE VIRGIN WOOL 8 OZ (224 G) 465 YD (425 M) SKEIN

1 skein #098 Natural (MC)

LION BRAND LION SUEDE 100% POLYESTER 3 OZS (85 G) 122 YARDS (110 M) BALL

1 ball #126 Coffee (CC) or color of your choice

- Size 9 (5.5 mm) knitting needles *or size to obtain gauge*
- ¼ yd (0.25 m) fabric for lining
- Size 16 blunt yarn needle
- Sewing needle and off-white thread

GAUGE

17 stitches + 25 rows = 4" (10 cm) in stockinette stitch (knit on right side, purl on wrong side) with MC, before felting.
Be sure to check your gauge.

BAG—MAKE 2

With MC, cast on 50 stitches. Work 90 rows in stockinette stitch. Bind off all stitches.

FELTING

Run the knit panels through your hottest wash cycle until knit panels have felted (at least 2 cycles).

Steam-press the panels flat. Felt pieces will not be perfect rectangles. Using a ruler, measure and mark a rectangle 8" (20.5 cm) across and 11" (28 cm) down. Cut off excess. Fold the top of the felt panels down 1" (2.5 cm) to right side and press.

TIES—MAKE 2

Cut 3 strands of CC, each 20" (51 cm) long, and knot together 2" (5 cm) from the top. Braid 3 strands together until 2" (5 cm) remains; knot together.

HANDLE

Cut strands of CC, each 40" (101.5 cm) long, and knot together 3" (7.5 cm) from the top. Divide into 3 parts and braid together until 3" (7.5 cm) remains; knot together.

LINING

Cut lining fabric to 7½" x 19½" (19 x 49.5 cm). Fold in half with right sides together and press. Fold the 2 top edges ½" (13 mm) to the wrong side and press. Place the wrong side of lining to wrong side of felt panels. Felt panels should have ½" (13 mm) allowances at bottom and top edges and ⅛" (3 mm) at each side edge. Place the Ties under the lining fold at center top edge and secure to felt with a couple of back stitches. Thread a long length of sewing thread and whipstitch lining to felt panels along the 2 top edges. Secure the bottom edge to 1 panel.

FINISHING

Thread a long length of CC and blanket stitch the cut end of the folded top edge. Secure yarn ends on the inside with a single knot. Baste the front and back of Bag together with sewing thread, then whipstitch along side and bottom seams. Stitches should be formed ½" (13 mm) from the edge and ½" (13 mm) apart (mark every ½" [13 mm] with a disappearing ink marking pen if needed). Whipstitch seams again to create the zigzag effect. Sew Handle to the top edge of Bag, matching knots with blanket stitching just under top edge.

FELTED CARRYALL

DESIGNED BY VIRGINIA ROWAN ROKHOLT

KNIT/EASY

Felting strengthens the knitted fabric enough to make it possible to create a supersize bag big enough for a day's essentials.

SIZE

Circumference 56" (142 cm) before felting; 43" (109 cm) after felting
Length 18" (45.5 cm) before felting; 9" (23 cm) after felting (excluding Handles)

MATERIALS

LION BRAND LANDSCAPES
50% WOOL, 50% ACRYLIC
1¾ OZ (50 G) 55 YD (50M) BALL

4 balls # 277 Country Sunset (A)
4 balls # 275 Autumn Trails (B)
4 balls # 273 Spring Desert (C)
or colors of your choice

- Size 13 (9 mm) 24" (60 cm) circular knitting needle *or size to obtain gauge*
- Stitch markers
- Large-eyed, blunt needle
- Size N-13 (9 mm) crochet hook

GAUGE

10.75 stitch + 12 rows = 4" (10 cm) in stockinette stitch (knit every round), before felting.
Be sure to check your gauge.

NOTE

Lion Brand Landscapes has an acrylic core wrapped with wool. When it is washed, the wool felts around the acrylic, which gives the finished item an interesting texture and appearance. However, it does not felt exactly like 100% wool and may take longer to felt than pure wool.

HANDLES—MAKE 2

With A, cast on 4 stitches.
Knit 4 rows; break off yarn, leaving a 6" (15 cm) tail. Cast on an additional 4 stitches to needle with original 4 stitches. Working only on new set of 4 stitches, knit 4 rows. Knit across all 8 stitches and work in garter stitch on all 8 stitches for 12" (30.5 cm). Knit 4 rows on first 4 stitches and bind off. Knit 4 rows on remaining 4 stitches and bind off. Fold Handle in half lengthwise and sew edge, leaving the 4-stitch tabs free.

TIES—MAKE 2

With A, cast on 34 stitches. Bind off immediately on next row.

BAG

BASE

Cut strands of A as follows to be used later in finishing: approximately 53 strands, each 5" (12.5 cm) long, for decorative Fringe; and 4 strands, each approximately 10" (25.5 cm), for sewing Handles and Ties.
With A, cast on 50 stitches, do not join. Work in garter stitch (knit every row) for 7" (18 cm). Do not break yarn.

BODY

Continuing with A, knit 50 stitches across row; pick up and knit 25 stitches down short edge of Base; pick up and knit 50 stitches on bottom edge of Base; pick up and knit 25 stitches down remaining short edge; place marker, and join, being careful not to twist—150 stitches. Work in stockinette stitch (knit every row) until all balls of A are finished; change to B and continue in stockinette stitch until all balls of B are finished; change to C. When Body measures 18" (45 cm) bind off loosely.

ASSEMBLY

Separate tabs at ends of each Handle, and place 1 tab on inside and other tab on outside of Bag; stitch securely to end of Bag. Weave in ends.

FRINGE

With crochet hook, attach Fringe as follows: Fold 1 strand in half to form loop. Insert crochet hook from right side through a stitch in 3rd row down from top of Bag and pull loop partway through. Tuck tails into loop and tighten against fabric of Bag. Continue around top of Bag, placing a Fringe strand approximately every 3rd or 4th stitch.

FELTING

Wash by machine on a hot wash/cold rinse cycle with detergent and several pieces of clothing to agitate. To felt additionally, dry by machine on regular setting until almost dry. Remove from dryer and lie flat to shape.

FINISHING

Sew ties securely to top edge of Bag.

IT FELT LIKE SPRING

DESIGNED BY VIRGINIA ROWAN ROKHOLT

KNIT/BEGINNER

This funky handbag incorporates a nonfelting yarn for additional color and texture. The faux tortoiseshell handles and felted fringe take a simple shape for a walk on the wild side.

SIZE

20" x 20" (51 x 51 cm) before felting; 11" x 6½" (28 x 16.5 cm) after felting

MATERIALS

LION BRAND LION WOOL
100% WOOL SOLIDS 3 OZ (85 G) 158 YARDS (144 M) PRINTS 2 OZ (78 G) 143 YARDS (131 M)

1 ball each #123 Sage (A) #202 Flower Garden (B) or colors of your choice

LION BRAND TRELLIS
100% NYLON 1 OZ (50 G)
115 YARDS (105 M)

1 ball #305 Stained Glass (C) or color of your choice

- Size 10.5 (6.5 mm) knitting needles *or size to obtain gauge*
- Size K-10.5 (6.5 mm) crochet hook
- Lucite tortoiseshell handles
- Large-eyed, blunt needle

GAUGE

16 stitches = 4" (10 cm) in stockinette stitch (knit on right side, purl on wrong side) with A before felting.
Be sure to check your gauge.

NOTE

Bag is knit in random stripes of A and B. Randomly work in yarn C by holding it together with A or B.

BAG

Cast on 80 stitches. Work in stockinette stitch, randomly striping yarns, until piece measures 40" (101.5 cm) from beginning. Bind off. Fold in half widthwise and crochet seams using a slip stitch. Weave in ends.

FRINGE

Cut 50 strands, each 5" (12.5 cm) long, of A and B. Use 1 strand for each Fringe. Fold strand in half to form a loop. Insert crochet hook into rim of Bag and draw loop through. Draw ends of Fringe through loop and tighten. Work evenly around rim of Bag and randomly throughout the piece for added texture.

FELTING

Felt Bag by running through a hot wash cycle with 1 tablespoon (15 ml) of detergent. Pull Bag into shape and let air dry. Repeat until Bag has reached desired size.

FINISHING

Sew Handles to inside of Bag rim. Fold up lower corners of Bag as shown and tack in place.

EASTER BASKET

DESIGNED BY VIRGINIA ROWAN ROKHOLT

KNIT/EASY

Give your sense of humor free rein while refining your felting technique. This fun little bag will steal the show at the egg hunt! Personalize your project with Fimo trinkets made from polymer clay.

SIZE

Circumference 40" (101.5 cm) before felting; 32" (81.5 cm) after felting
Height 14" (35.5 cm) before felting; 7" (18 cm) after felting, excluding Handles

MATERIALS

LION BRAND LANDSCAPES
50% WOOL, 50% ACRYLIC
$1^{3}/_{4}$ OZ (50 G) 55 YD (50 M) BALL

5 balls #272 Pastel Meadow (A) or color of your choice

LION BRAND WOOL-EASE
80% ACRYLIC, 20% WOOL
3 OZ (85 G) 197 YD (187 M) BALL

1 ball #175 Green (B) or color of your choice

- Size 13 (9 mm) knitting needles *or size to obtain gauge*
- Size 13 (9 mm) 29" (70 cm) circular needle
- Crochet hook (for attaching fringe)
- Stitch markers
- Orange polymer clay (such as Fimo or Sculpey)
- Glue gun and glue sticks
- Large-eyed, blunt needle

GAUGE

12 stitches + 16 rounds = 4" (10 cm) in stockinette stitch (knit every round) with A before felting.
Be sure to check your gauge.

NOTE

Lion Brand Landscapes has an acrylic core wrapped with wool. When it is washed, the wool felts around the acrylic, which gives the finished item an interesting texture and appearance. However, it does not felt exactly like 100% wool and may take longer to felt than pure wool.

BASKET

BASE

With A, cast on 36 stitches. Work in garter stitch (Knit every row) until piece measures 8" (20.5 cm) from beg.

SIDES

With circular needle, knit 36 stitches; pick up and knit 24 stitches along side edge of Base, 36 stitches across cast-on edge, and 24 stitches along 2nd side edge of Base—120 stitches. Place marker for beginning of round. Change to stockinette stitch and work even until piece measures $13^{1}/_{2}$" (34.5 cm) from Base. Purl 3 rounds. Bind off.

HANDLES—MAKE 2

With A, cast on 4 stitches. Knit 4

rows. With a separate strand of A, cast on 4 stitches onto same needle. Knit 4 rows. Working across all 8 stitches, work in garter stitch until piece measures 8" (20.5 cm) from beginning. Working on 4 stitches only, knit 4 rows. Bind off these 4 stitches. Join yarn to remaining 4 stitches. Knit 4 rows. Bind off.

Fold Handle in half lengthwise and sew center part of Handle together. Sew Handles to basket by placing 1 section at bottom of handle and sewing to inside of basket, and sewing the other section to outside of basket. Weave in ends.

FRINGE

Cut 50 strands of A, each 8" (20.5 cm) long. Fold strand in half to form a loop. Insert crochet hook into edge of basket and draw loop through. Draw ends of Fringe through loop and tighten. Place Fringe, evenly spaced, around top edge of basket.

FELTING

Felt basket by running through a hot wash cycle with 1 tablespoon (15 ml) of detergent. Pull basket into shape and let air dry. Repeat until stitches are indistinguishable and Basket has reached desired size.

TIES—MAKE 2

With A, cast on 34 stitches. Bind off. Sew to either side at center of top edge of Basket.

CARROTS

Following polymer clay directions, make 9 Carrots. Cut 27 random lengths of B, between 1½" and 3" (3.8 and 7.5 cm), and 9 strands 7" (18 cm) long of B. With glue gun, attach yarn to tops of Carrots, making sure each Carrot has a 7" (18 cm) length. Thread each 7" (18 cm) length through to the inside of Basket and knot to secure each Carrot.

LOOPY TOTEBAG

DESIGNED BY VIRGINIA ROWAN ROKHOLT

KNIT/EASY

Hard Lucite handles lend a deco touch to this soft, felted tote, while loopy trim adds girlish whimsy. Smart yet practical, it makes a fun, feminine fashion statement.

SIZE

Before felting 20" tall x 25" wide (51 x 63.5 cm), excluding handles
After felting 10" tall x 16" wide (25.5 x 40.5 cm), excluding Handles

MATERIALS

LION BRAND FISHERMEN'S WOOL 100% PURE VIRGIN WOOL 8 OZ (224 G) 465 YD (425 M) SKEIN

2 skeins #098 Natural

- Size 10.5 (6.5 mm) knitting needles *or size to obtain gauge*
- Size 8 (5 mm) double-pointed needles
- Size G-6 (4 mm) crochet hook
- Lucite handles
- 1 yard (1 m) leopard-print ribbon (sample uses Offray # 310054)
- Glue gun
- Glue sticks
- Large-eyed, blunt needle

GAUGE

14.5 stitches = 4" [10 cm] in stockinette stitch (knit on right side, purl on wrong side) on larger needle before felting.
Be sure to check your gauge.

BAG

With larger needles, cast on 90 stitches. Work in stockinette stitch for 40" (101.5 cm). Bind off. Fold in half widthwise with wrong sides together. Using crochet hook, slip stitch side seams together.

RUFFLES

With double-pointed needles, cast on 6 stitches. *Slide stitches to other end of double-pointed needle and knit them, pulling yarn tightly across the back of the work. (Do not turn work.) Repeat from * until cord measures 20 feet (6 m). With crochet hook, use slip stitch to attach cord around opening of Bag, making the loops approximately 6–7" (15–18 cm) long.

FELTING

Wash by machine on a hot wash/cold rinse cycle with detergent and several pieces of clothing to agitate. To felt additionally, dry by machine on a regular setting until almost dry. Remove from dryer and lay flat to shape.

FINISHING

Thread large-eyed, blunt needle with yarn and sew handles securely to top of Bag. Fold lower corners up as shown and tack in place. Cut ribbon in half and glue to center points at top of Bag. Tie in bow.

PAMPERED PUPPY

DESIGNED BY CATHY MAGUIRE

KNIT/INTERMEDIATE

Bring your pooch on a sleepover or carry her around town—this bag works as a doggie bed or carrier.

SIZE

8" x 12" x 8" (20 x 30.5 x 20 cm)

MATERIALS

LION BRAND LION WOOL
100% WOOL
3 OZ (85 G) 158 YD (144 M)

4 balls #113 Scarlet (MC)
1 ball #099 Winter White (CC)
or colors of your choice

- Size 9 (5.5 mm) knitting needles *or size to obtain gauge*
- Contrasting-colored, smooth yarn to be used as waste yarn
- Stitch holders
- 1¼ yd [1.25 m] ¼" [19 mm] cotton twill tape
- Two 8" x 12" (20 x 30.5 cm) sheets plastic canvas mesh (gauge 10)
- #16 blunt yarn needle
- 2½ yd (2.5 m) 1" (2.5 cm) nylon webbing in navy
- Sewing thread in navy
- Perle cotton in cream

GAUGE

16 stitches + 22 rows = 4" (10 cm) in stockinette stitch (knit on right side, purl on wrong side) before felting.
Be sure to check your gauge.

NOTE

Two bag pieces are knit in stockinette stitch. Both side panel and front panel overlap at the bottom (2 layers) and plastic canvas in inserted in between the bottom layers. Side seams are sewn with an invisible stitch. Top edge has a double hem. Webbing is machine or hand sewn to make handles.

SIDE PANEL

With waste yarn, cast on 75 stitches and knit 4 rows. Join MC.
Rows 1–69 Work in stockinette stitch.
Row 70 Bind off 1 stitch, work to end of row—74 stitches. Cut MC and join CC.
Row 71 Bind off 1 stitch, work to end of row—73 stitches. Cut CC and join MC.
Rows 72–151 Work in stockinette stitch. After Row 151, cut MC and join CC.
Row 152 Work in stockinette stitch. Cut CC and join MC.
Rows 153–154 Cast on 1 stitch, work to end of row—75 stitches after Row 154.
Rows 155–222 Work in stockinette stitch. After Row 222, cut MC and join CC.

Rows 223–224 Work in stockinette stitch. After Row 224, cut CC and join MC.
Rows 225–245 Work in stockinette stitch.
Place stitches on holder.
Carefully remove waste yarn and place 75 stitches on needle.
Join CC and work 2 rows in stockinette stitch. Cut CC and join MC.
Work 20 rows in stockinette stitch.
Place stitches on holder.

FRONT/BACK PANEL

With waste yarn, cast on 50 stitches. Knit 4 rows. Join MC.
Rows 1–69 Work in stockinette stitch.
Row 70 Bind off 1 stitch, work to end of row—49 stitches. Cut MC and join CC.
Row 71 Bind off 1 stitch, work to end of row—48 stitches. Cut CC and join MC.
Rows 72–192 Work in stockinette stitch. After Row 192, cut MC and join CC.
Row 193 Work in stockinette stitch. Cut CC and join MC.
Rows 194–195 Cast on 1 stitch, work to end of row—50 stitches after Row 195.
Rows 196–220 Work in stockinette stitch.
Row 221 Knit 12 with MC; join CC and knit 26, weaving MC across WS; knit 12 with MC.
Row 222 Purl 12 with MC; p 26 with CC, weaving MC across WS; purl 12 with MC. Cut CC.
Rows 223–232 Work in stockinette stitch.

DOGGIE OPENING

RIGHT SIDE

Row 233 Knit 12; place remaining stitches on holder.
Rows 234–263 Work in stockinette stitch. After Row 263, cut MC and join CC.
Rows 264–265 Work in stockinette stitch. After Row 265, cut CC and join MC.
Rows 266–286 Work in stockinette stitch.
Place stitches on holder.

LEFT SIDE

Place last 12 stitches from holder onto needle, ready to work a RS row; join MC.
Repeat Rows 233–286 of right side.
Place stitches on holder.

CENTER

Place center 26 stitches on needle.
Join MC and work 10 rows in stockinette stitch. Bind off.
Carefully remove waste yarn and place 50 stitches on needle.
Join CC and work 2 rows stockinette stitch. Cut CC and join MC.
Work 20 rows in stockinette stitch.
Place stitches on holder.

FINISHING

Place wrong side of Front/Back Panel over right side of Side Panel crosswise—centers of pieces overlap to form base. Sew 4 side seams from base to top. **Note** The overlapping bases will not match up until they are felted.

HEM

Beginning at left of Center opening, work Hem across all 224 stitches as follows:
Fold the last 20 rows to the inside so that the stitches line up with the top of the CC row. Knit 1, *with left needle, pick up first stitch in CC row and knit, knit 1 on needle, pass first 2 stitches over 3rd stitch (1 stitch on right needle). Repeat from * until all stitches have been worked. Fasten off last stitch.
Cut a 37" (94 cm) length of twill tape and insert through Hem with a large safety pin. Tack to ends of opening. The twill will gather the

Hem but will help it felt to correct dimensions.

FELTING

Put the finished Bag through the hottest wash cycle twice. After the second wash, felt should be pliable enough to manipulate the two bottom panels to measure 8" x 12" (20 x 30.5 cm). Steam if necessary. Readjust the twill between washes so that sides measure 8" x 12" (20 x 30.5 cm).

BASE

Place one plastic canvas piece on top of the other and secure with a few stitches. Insert between the 2 bottom layers of the Bag. Whipstitch all 4 sides of base to plastic canvas, using the CC rows as guides. Pinch each corner of the top edge of Bag and whipstitch a few times. Put the Bag through the wash cycle one or two more times. Remove twill tape.

WEBBING STRAPS

Join the 2½ yard (2.5 m) of webbing by overlapping and securing with a few rows of stitches to form a closed ring. Fold flat at seam and use seam as a mark, then place the second (halfway) mark at opposite fold. You now have a 90" (228.5 cm) ring divided in half with the seam and halfway mark.

Place webbing across base, parallel to and 2" (5 cm) from the front edge. Center the webbing seam (4" [10 cm] from each side) and pin in place at center and sides. Repeat for the other end, centering the halfway mark 2" (5 cm) from the back edge. Continue to pin webbing up the sides of the bag, 2" (5 cm) from the front and back edges. Tack webbing in place using sewing thread. Topstitch webbing edges with cream perle cotton.

7.

NEW BAG OF TRICKS

This chapter brings all your new skills together. When you've mastered crochet you can go wild with a free-form bag or construct a sculptural circle-handle bag. If you can knit and crochet, the crocheted tote with (knitted) felt handles and trim is a challenge you can accept and a great way of showing off all your skills—knitting, crocheting, felting, lining, and top-stitching. If you're looking for a novel piece, the Coffee Cup Bag is a fun, one-of-a-kind project.

FREE-FORM BAG

DESIGNED BY SHEILA PEPE

CROCHET/INTERMEDIATE

This bag showcases the unique design skills and color sensibilities of noted crochet artist and sculptor Sheila Pepe. This project is an opportunity to expand your technique and style.

SIZE

15" wide x 9½" tall (38 x 24 cm), excluding Strap

MATERIALS

LION BRAND GLITTERSPUN 60% ACRYLIC, 13% POLYESTER, 27% CUPRO 1¾ OZ (50 G) 115 YD (105 M) BALL

2 balls #153 Onyx (A) or color of your choice

LION BRAND HOMESPUN 98% ACRYLIC, 2% POLYESTER 6 OZ (170 G) 185 YD (167 M) SKEIN

1 skein #312 Edwardian (B) or color of your choice

LION BRAND WOOL-EASE CHUNKY 80% ACRYLIC, 20% WOOL 5 OZ (140 G) 153 YD (140 M) BALL

1 ball #107 Bluebell (C) or color of your choice

LION BRAND FUN FUR 100% POLYESTER 1¾ OZ (50 G) 64 YD (58 M) BALL

1 ball #132 Olive (D) or color of your choice

- Size G-6 (4 mm) crochet hook *or size to obtain gauge*
- Size H-8 (5 mm) crochet hook *or size to obtain gauge*
- Size I-9 (5.5 mm) crochet hook *or size to obtain gauge*
- Scraps of contrasting yarn to be used as markers
- Large-eyed, blunt needle

GAUGE

16 single crochet + 20 rows = 4" (10 cm) with A on smallest hook.
10 single crochet + 12 rows = 4" (10 cm) with B on middle-sized hook.
First 3 rounds of Bottom = 2" (5 cm) across.
Be sure to check your gauge.

STITCH EXPLANATION

Stitch 2 together (single crochet decrease) Insert hook into stitch and draw up a loop. Insert hook into next stitch and draw up a loop. Yarn over, draw through all 3 loops on hook.

NOTE

This is a free-form design, composed of a Bottom, 2 Gussets, a Front, and a Back worked in rows to fit between the Gussets, a circular Flap, a Strap, and Trim Rows that are added later. The materials used vary in gauge, and stitch count may need to be adjusted to keep work flat. The beauty of a free-form design is the uniqueness of each piece. Feel free to be creative and adjust your stitches to fit your own piece.

BOTTOM

Starting at bottom, with largest hook and A, chain 36.

Round 1 (Wrong Side) Single crochet in 2nd chain from hook and in each chain across to last chain, 3 single crochet in last chain; working across opposite side of foundation chain, single crochet in each chain across to last chain, 2 single crochet in last chain. Do not join. Work in a spiral, marking first stitch of each round, moving marker up as work progresses—74 single crochet.

Round 2 2 single crochet in next single crochet, single crochet in each of next 34 single crochet, 2 single crochet in each of next 3 single crochet, single crochet in each of next 34 single crochet, 2 single crochet in each of next 2 single crochet—80 single crochet.

Round 3 Single crochet in each single crochet around.

Round 4 *Single crochet in next single crochet, 2 single crochet in next single crochet, single crochet in each of next 34 single crochet, [single crochet in next single crochet, 2 single crochet in next single crochet] twice; repeat from * once—86 single crochet.

Round 5 Single crochet in each single crochet around.

Round 6 *Single crochet in next 2 single crochet, 2 single crochet in next single crochet, single crochet in each of next 34 single crochet, [sc in next 2 single crochet, 2 single crochet in next sc] twice. Repeat from * once—92 single crochet.

Round 7 *Single crochet in next 3 single crochet, 2 single crochet in next single crochet, single crochet in each of next 34 single crochet, [single crochet in next 3 single crochet, 2 single crochet in next single crochet] twice. Repeat from * once—98 single crochet.

Rounds 8–10 Single crochet in each single crochet around. At end of Round 10, join with slip stitch in next single crochet.

Round 11 Chain 1, single crochet in each single crochet around, working single crochet 2 together 3 times evenly spaced across each end of oval—92 single crochet.

Round 12 Chain 1, single crochet in each single crochet around, working single crochet 2 together 4 times evenly spaced across each end of oval—84 single crochet.

Rounds 13–15 Chain 3, double crochet in each stitch around. Join with slip stitch in top of beginning chain—84 stitches.

Place a marker in each of Rounds 13–15.

Round 16 Chain 1, single crochet in each stitch around. Join with slip stitch in first single crochet.

Round 17 Chain 4, skip next single crochet, *double crochet in next single crochet, chain 1, skip next single crochet; repeat from * around. Join with slip stitch in 3rd chain of beginning chain—42 chain 1-spaces. Fasten off A. Place a marker in this round.

GUSSETS

Note Gussets are now added at each end of Bottom. Front and Back are worked in rows, joining to Gussets at each end of each row.

FIRST GUSSET

Turn Bottom inside out so that wrong side is facing.

With smallest hook, join A in center chain 1-space on one end of Bottom; chain 14.

Row 1 Single crochet in 2nd chain from hook and in each chain across, slip stitch in next double crochet in Round 17, slip stitch in next chain 1-space. Turn—13 single crochet.

Row 2 Single crochet in each single crochet across, 3 single crochet in end chain 1-space; working across opposite side of foundation chain, single crochet in each chain across, slip stitch in next double crochet in Round 17—29 single crochet. Fasten off.

SECOND GUSSET

With smallest hook, join A in center chain 1-space on opposite end of Bottom. Chain 19.

Row 1 Single crochet in 2nd chain from hook and in each chain across, slip stitch in next double crochet in Round 17, slip stitch in next chain 1-space. Turn—18 single crochet.

Row 2 Single crochet in each single crochet across, 3 single crochet in end chain 1-space; working across opposite side of foundation chain, single crochet in each chain across, slip stitch in next double crochet in Round 17—39 single crochet. Fasten off.

FRONT

Row 1 (Right Side) With wrong side of Bottom facing and middle-sized hook, join B in first chain 1-space to the left of First Gusset (shorter Gusset), chain 3, double crochet in same chain 1-space, double crochet in each chain 1-space across to Second Gusset (longer Gusset), single crochet in 2nd single crochet of Gusset, single crochet in next single crochet, slip stitch in next single crochet. Turn—22 stitches.

Row 2 Chain 1, *single crochet in each double crochet across, single crochet in next 2 single crochet on Gusset, slip stitch in next single crochet. Turn—24 single crochet.

Round 3 Chain 1, single crochet in each single crochet across, single crochet in each of next 3 single crochet on Gusset, slip stitch in next single crochet. Turn—27 single crochet.

Row 4 Chain 1, single crochet in each single crochet across, single crochet in next single crochet on Gusset, slip stitch in next single crochet. Turn—28 single crochet.

Row 5 Chain 1, single crochet in each single crochet across, single crochet in each of next 3 single crochet on Gusset, slip stitch in next single crochet. Turn—31 single crochet.

Row 6 Chain 1, single crochet in each single crochet across, single crochet in each of next 2 single crochet of Gusset, slip stitch in next. Turn—33 single crochet.

Row 7 Chain 1, single crochet in each single crochet across, single crochet in each of next 3 single crochet on Gusset, slip stitch in next single crochet. Turn—36 single crochet.

Row 8 Chain 1, single crochet in each single crochet across, single crochet in next single crochet of Gusset, slip stitch in each of next 2 single crochet on Gusset. Turn—37 single crochet.

Row 9 Do not chain 1, single crochet in each single crochet across, single crochet in each of next 3 single crochet on Gusset, slip stitch in next single crochet. Turn—40 single crochet. Fasten off B.

Top edge of Front should align with tops of Gussets. If necessary, continue to work in rows of single crochet, slip stitch in Gusset at end of each row, until Front aligns with tops of Gussets.

BACK

Turn Bag right side out. With right side of Bottom facing and middle-sized hook, join B in first chain 1-space to the left of First Gusset (shorter Gusset), chain 3, double crochet in same chain 1-space, double crochet in each chain

1-space across to Second Gusset (longer Gusset), single crochet in 2nd single crochet of Gusset, single crochet in next single crochet, slip stitch in next single crochet. Turn—22 stitches.

Rows 2–6 Repeat Rows 2–6 of Front. Fasten off B. Join C.

Rows 7–9 With C, repeat Rows 7–9 of Front. Fasten off C.

TOP BORDER

Round 1 With right side of Front facing and smallest hook, join A in top of First Gusset (shorter Gusset), chain 1, single crochet evenly spaced around Front and Back, increasing as necessary to keep work flat. Join with slip stitch in first single crochet.

Round 2 chain 1, single crochet in each single crochet around. Join with slip stitch in first single crochet. Fasten off A.

FLAP

With C, chain 2.

Round 1 (Right Side) Work 6 single crochet in 2nd chain from hook. Do not join. Work in a spiral, marking beginning of each round, moving marker up as work progresses—6 single crochet.

Round 2 [single crochet, chain 1] in each single crochet around—6 chain 1-spaces.

Round 3 [single crochet, chain 1] in each single crochet and each chain 1-space around—12 chain 1-spaces.

Round 4 *[single crochet, chain 1] in each of next 3 chain 1-spaces, [single crochet, chain 1, single crochet, chain 1] in next chain 1-space. Repeat from * around—15 chain 1-spaces.

Round 5 *[single crochet, chain 1] in each of next 2 chain 1-spaces, [single crochet, chain 1, single crochet, chain 1] in next chain 1-space. Repeat from * around—20 chain 1-spaces. Fasten off C. Join B.

Round 6 With B, single crochet in each single crochet and each chain 1-space around—40 single crochet.

Note Work now progresses in rows across bottom edge of Flap.

Row 7 Single crochet in each of next 14 single crochet. Turn—14 single crochet.

Rows 8–9 Chain 1, single crochet in each single crochet across. Turn. Fasten off B.

FLAP EDGING

Round 1 With right side facing and smallest hook, join A in any single crochet; chain 1, single crochet in each single crochet and each row-end single crochet around. Join with slip stitch in first sc—46 single crochet. Fasten off.

ASSEMBLY

With right side of Flap and Back facing, position top edge of Flap (edge with only 1 round of B) centered on Top Border (does not need to be exact). With large-eyed, blunt needle and A, sew center 6 stitches of Flap to corresponding stitches on Top Edging of Back.

FLAP TRIM

Row 1 With right side of Flap facing and smallest hook, leaving a tail for sewing, join A in first free single crochet on Top Border to the right of Flap. Turn to work around Flap, single crochet in each of first 3 single crochet on Flap Edging, chain 1, [double crochet, chain 1] in each single crochet around to last 3 stitches before joining, single crochet in each of next 3 single crochet, slip stitch in corresponding single crochet in Top Border. Fasten off, leaving a tail for sewing. With tails, sew last 3 stitches of last row to corresponding stitches on Top Border.

CONTINUE TOP BORDER

Row 1 With right side facing, join D in first single crochet on Top Border to the left of last slip stitch made in Flap Trim. Chain 1, single crochet in each single crochet around to opposite side of Flap Trim. Turn. Fasten off D.

Row 2 With wrong side facing, join B in first single crochet, chain 1, single crochet in each single crochet across, slip stitch in next 2 single crochet on Flap Trim. Turn. Do not fasten off. Place a marker at each end of center 6 stitches on Front.

TOP LEFT CORNER

Row 1 (Right Side) Single crochet in each single crochet across Top Border to first marker. Turn.

Row 2 Chain 1, single crochet 2 together in first 2 stitches, single crochet in each single crochet across to last 2 stitches, single crochet 2 together in last 2 stitches, slip stitch in next 2 stitches on Flap Trim. Turn.

Row 3 Chain 1, single crochet 2 together in first 2 stitches, single crochet in each single crochet across to last 2 stitches, single crochet 2 together in last 2 stitches. Turn.

Rows 4–5 Repeat Rows 2–3, adjusting stitches as necessary on Flap side to keep work flat. Fasten off B.

TOP RIGHT CORNER

Row 1 (Right Side) With right side facing, join B in first stitch to the left of 2nd marked stitch on Front, chain 1, single crochet 2 together in next 2 stitches, single crochet in each single crochet across to last 2 stitches before Flap Trim, single crochet 2 together in last 2 stitches, slip stitch in next 2 stitches on Flap Trim. Turn.

Row 2 Chain 1, single crochet 2 together in first 2 stitches, single crochet in each single crochet across to last 2 stitches, single crochet 2 together in last 2 stitches. Turn.

Row 3 Chain 1, single crochet 2 together in first 2 stitches, single crochet in each single crochet across to last 2 stitches, single crochet 2 together in last 2 stitches, slip stitch in next 2 stitches on Flap Trim. Turn.

Rows 4–5 Repeat Rows 2–3, adjusting stitches as necessary on Flap side to keep work flat. Fasten off B.

TOP TRIM

Row 1 With right side of Back facing, flatten Bag, making folds directly above Gussets. Join A in top right corner. Working through double thickness, with smallest hook, chain 1, single crochet evenly spaced across to Flap; working in single thickness, single crochet in each double crochet and chain 1-space across Flap Edging; working across top left side, working through double thickness of Front and Back, single crochet evenly spaced across to corner. Fasten off A.

FRONT TRIM

Row 1 With right side facing and smallest hook, join A in first free stitch on Front Edge, chain 1, single crochet evenly spaced across Front Edge. Fasten off.

STRAP

With A, chain 150, or 4" (10 cm) less than desired length.

Round 1 Single crochet in 2nd chain from hook and in each chain across to last chain, 3 single crochet in last chain. Place a marker in first of these 3 single crochet. Working across opposite side of foundation chain, single crochet in each chain across to last chain, 2 single crochet in last chain, slip stitch in first single crochet.

Round 2 Chain 1, 2 single crochet in first single crochet, single crochet in each single crochet across to marked stitch, 2 single crochet in each of next 3 single crochet, single crochet in each single crochet across to last 2 single crochet, 2 single crochet in each of last 2 single crochet. Join with slip stitch in first single crochet. Fasten off, leaving a tail for sewing.

FINISHING

Lay one end of Strap over fold on one end of Bag, positioned about 2" (5 cm) below top edge. Sew end of Strap in place. Without twisting Strap, position and sew other end of Strap to opposite side of Bag.

TRIM ROW 1

With right side facing and Bottom on top, join B around the post of first double crochet in first marked row near Bottom of Bag. Chain 1, single crochet around the post of each double crochet around. Fasten off.

TRIM ROW 2

Repeat Trim Row 1 in 2nd marked row from bottom.

TRIM ROW 3

With C, repeat Trim Row 1 in 3rd marked row from bottom.

TRIM ROW 4

With D, repeat Trim Row 1 in 4th marked row from bottom.

Weave in ends.

CIRCLE IN THE SQUARE BAG

DESIGNED BY VLADIMIR TERIOKHIN

KNIT WITH CROCHET HANDLES/EASY

Knit and crochet come together to make a simple, modern bag with built-in handles.

SIZE

9" wide x 13" tall (23 x 33 cm), including Handles

MATERIALS

LION BRAND CHENILLE THICK & QUICK 91% ACRYLIC, 9% RAYON 100 YD (90 M) SKEIN

1 skein each #131 Forest Green (A) #178 Basil (B) or colors of your choice

- Size 11 (8 mm) knitting needles *or size to obtain gauge*
- Size P-15 (10 mm) crochet hook *or size to obtain gauge*
- Large-eyed, blunt needle

GAUGE

9 stitches + 12 rows = 4" (10 cm) in stockinette stitch (knit on right side, purl on wrong side).
9 single crochet + 9 rows = 4" (10 cm).
Be sure to check your gauge.

KNIT BASE

With A, cast on 22 stitches. Work 24 rows in stockinette stitch. Bind off all stitches.

CROCHET HANDLES—MAKE 2

With B, Chain 35. Join with slip stitch to form ring.

Round 1 Chain 3 (counts as 1 double crochet), 39 double crochet in ring. Join with slip stitch in top of beginning chain. Turn—40 stitches.

Round 2 Chain 3, double crochet in same stitch, [double crochet in next 8 stitches, 2 double crochet in each of next 2 stitches] 3 times, double crochet in next 8 stitches, 2 double crochet in next stitch. Join with slip stitch in top of beginning chain. Turn—48 stitches.

Row 3 Chain 1, single crochet in same stitch, [single crochet in next 10 stitches, 2 single crochet in each of next 2 stitches] 2 times, single crochet in next 11 stitches. Turn, leaving remaining stitches unworked—40 stitches.

Row 4 Chain 1, single crochet in same stitches, [single crochet in next 12 stitches, 2 single crochet in each of next 2 stitches] 2 times, single crochet in next 11 stitches—44 stitches. Fasten off.

FINISHING

Narrow section of Handle is top edge. Sew bottom edge of one Handle to bound-off edge of base, and bottom edge of 2nd Handle to cast-on edge. Fold piece with right sides together, joining handles. Sew side seams.

TOP EDGING

Join B at side seam.

Row 1 Chain 1, work 36 single crochet evenly spaced around opening. Join with slip stitch to beginning chain. Do not turn.

Row 2 chain 1, working from left to right, reverse single crochet in each single crochet around. Fasten off. Weave in ends.

FELT-TRIM TOTE

DESIGNED BY CATHY MAGUIRE

CROCHET WITH KNIT TRIM/INTERMEDIATE

Combine all of your skills—knitting, crocheting, mixing color, blending yarns, and felting—to create a sophisticated classic. The reinforced lining makes it strong enough for the long haul.

SIZE

13¼" wide x 13½" tall x 5¾" deep (33.5 x 34.5 x 14.5 cm), excluding Handles

MATERIALS

LION BRAND LION COTTON 100% COTTON SOLIDS 5 OZS (140 GMS) 236 YARDS (212 M) PRINTS 4 OZS (112 GMS) 189 YARDS (170 M)

2 balls each #098 Natural (A) #214 Naturals and Denim (B) or colors of your choice

LION BRAND LION BOUCLÉ 79% ACRYLIC. 20% MOHAIR, 2% NYLON 2½ OZ (70 G) 57 YD (52 M) BALL

1 ball #213 Taffy (C) or color of your choice

LION BRAND FISHERMEN'S WOOL 100% PURE VIRGIN WOOL 8 OZ (226 G) 465 YD (425 M) SKEIN

1 skein #098 Natural (D)

- Size N-13 (9 mm) crochet hook *or size to obtain gauge*
- Size 8 (5 mm) 29" (70 cm) circular needle
- Size 8 (5 mm) double-pointed needles
- Scraps of contrasting yarn to be used as markers
- 2 sheets plastic canvas mesh in gauge 10
- ½ yd (0.5 m) unbleached cotton muslin
- 1 pack Orbit Drip Master ¼" (6 mm) Soaker Tubing
- Off-white sewing machine thread
- Large-eyed, blunt needle

GAUGE

9 single crochet + 10 rows = 4" (10 cm) with 1 strand each of A and B or 1 strand each of B and C held together. *Be sure to check your gauge.*

NOTE

Front, bottom, and back are worked in 1 piece in 2-row stripes. Carry unused colors loosely along side edge.

TOTE

Starting at top edge of front, with 1 strand each of A and B held together, chain 31.

Row 1 (Right Side) Single crochet in 2nd chain from hook and in each chain across. Turn—30 single crochet.

Row 2 Chain 1, single crochet in each single crochet across. Turn. Drop A. Join 1 strand of C.

Row 3 With 1 strand each of B and C held together, chain 1, single crochet in each single crochet across. Turn.

Rows 4–82 Work even in single crochet in the following color sequence: 1 more row with B and C; *2 rows with A and B; 2 rows with B and C; repeat from * throughout. Mark beginning and end of Rows 34 and 47 to identify bottom of Tote. Fasten off.

SIDE PANEL

Row 1 With right side of Tote facing, join 1 strand each of A and B in first marked stitch on one side edge of Tote, chain 1, single crochet in each of next 13 row-end stitches to next marker. Turn—13 single crochet.

Rows 2–34 Work even on 13 single crochet, maintaining established color sequence. Fasten off.

Repeat Side Panel on opposite side of Tote.

With right sides together, using large-eyed, blunt needle and B, sew side seams. Weave in ends.

PLASTIC CANVAS HALF LINING

Cut 3 rectangles, each 5½" x 13½" (14 x 34.5 cm) of plastic canvas. Cut a piece of muslin 12" x 42" (30.5 x 106.5 cm). Fold in half lengthwise forming a 6" x 42" (15 x 106.5 cm) folded piece. Sew an L-shaped ¼" (6 mm) seam across the bottom 6"

(15 cm) and along the 42" (106.5 cm) long side. Turn right side out and press. Slip 1 plastic canvas rectangle inside pocket and push to the end. Sew a line of stitching to secure in place. Slip another plastic canvas rectangle inside pocket and push to the line of stitching. Sew a line of stitching to secure in place. Slip the last plastic canvas rectangle inside pocket and push to the second line of stitching. Fold on seam allowance and topstitch or whipstitch closed. Place lining to fit bottom and sides of Tote and tack or slip stitch in place.

KNIT HANDLES—MAKE 2

With double-pointed needles and D, cast on 8 stitches.
Row 1 (Knit 1, purl 1) across.
Row 2 (Purl 1, knit 1) across.
Repeat Rows 1–2 for 7 more times.
Row 17 Knit 1, knit 2 together, knit 2, knit 2 together, knit 1—6 stitches.
Join for working in the round. Knit 80 rounds.
Row 98 Turn work to begin knitting back and forth. Purl 1, purl into front and back of next stitch, purl 2, purl into front and back of next stitch, purl 1—8 stitches.
Rows 99–114 Repeat Rows 1–2.
Bind off.

VERTICAL STRIPS—MAKE 2

With D, cast on 6 stitches.
Row 1 (Knit 1, purl 1) across.
Row 2 (Purl 1, knit 1) across.
Repeat Rows 1–2 for 89 more times. Bind off.

HORIZONTAL STRIP—MAKE 1

With circular needle and D, cast on 144 stitches.
Row 1 (Knit 1, purl 1) across.
Row 2 (Purl 1, knit 1) across.
Repeat Rows 1–2 for 5 more times.
Bind off.

FELTING

Cut 2 lengths 20" (51 cm) of the soaker tubing and pull the Handles over the tubing before felting. They will be cut down to approximately 15" (38 cm) after the felting. The handles should be adjusted and pushed tighter up the tubing during wash cycles. Put the knit Strips and Handles through the hottest wash cycle at least twice until knit panels have felted. The Handles may need a third wash. Steam-press the flat panels. Pin the Vertical Strips to the Tote along the Front, Bottom, and Back. The outside edge of the Strip should line up with the outside edge of the Tote. Trim the Strip if it is too long. It's felted, so it won't run or rip. Sew both edges of the Strips to the Tote with B, using a running stitch. The stitches and gaps should both be 1⁄4" (6 mm) wide. Pin the Horizontal Strip to fit. You might need to stretch it to fit in the ease. Sew both edges with a running stitch all the way around the Tote. Pin the bottom of the Handles to the top of the Tote about 4" (10 cm) from the top of the Tote and 1 1⁄4" (3 cm) from the Vertical Strip. Sew a rectangle of running stitches to secure to Tote. Weave in ends.

COFFEE CUP BAG

DESIGNED BY BONNIE FRANZ

KNIT/INTERMEDIATE

Trompe l'oeil meets knitting in this witty translation of a New York icon.

SIZE

Circumference 18" (45.5 cm)
Height 9" (23 cm), excluding Drawstring

MATERIALS

LION BRAND LION COTTON 100% COTTON SOLIDS 5 OZS (140 GMS) 236 YARDS (212 M) PRINTS 4 OZS (112 GMS) 189 YARDS (170 M)

1 ball each #108 Morning Glory Blue (MC) #098 Natural (CC) or colors of your choice

- Size 7 (4.5 mm) 16" (40.5 cm) circular needle *or size to obtain gauge*
- Size 7 (4.5 mm) double-pointed needles
- Large-eyed, blunt needle

GAUGE

16 stitches + 24 rounds = 4" (10 cm) in stockinette stitch (knit every round).

Be sure to check your gauge.

STITCH EXPLANATION

Knitted cord Cast on desired number of stitches onto double–pointed needle. Knit all stitches. *Slide stitches to right end of needle. Without turning work, knit all stitches. Repeat from * until cord is desired length.
Note A spool knitter may also be used to create knitted cord.

BAG

With MC, work 4–stitch knitted cord for 62" (157.5 cm). Coil this cord into a flat disk approximately 5 1/2" (14 cm) in diameter and sew to secure. With MC and circular needle, pick up and knit 72 stitches around outer edge of coil. Knit, following chart. When 48 rounds of chart have been completed, work eyelet round.
Eyelet Round *Bind off 2 stitches, knit 7; repeat from * across row.
Next Round Knit, casting on 2 stitches over each eyelet—72 stitches.
With MC, work 5 more rounds in stockinette stitch. Bind off.

DRAWSTRING—MAKE 2

With MC, cast on 3 stitches. Work 3–stitch knitted cord for 48" (122 cm). Bind off.

FINISHING

Lace Drawstrings through eyelets and sew ends of each cord together. Split a 12" (30.5 cm) length of MC into two 2-ply pieces and use to embroider coffee cup handles and steam as shown on chart. Weave in ends. For added stability, the bottom of a plastic bottle (such as a juice bottle) can be placed in the bottom of the Bag.

sandwiches
seasonal

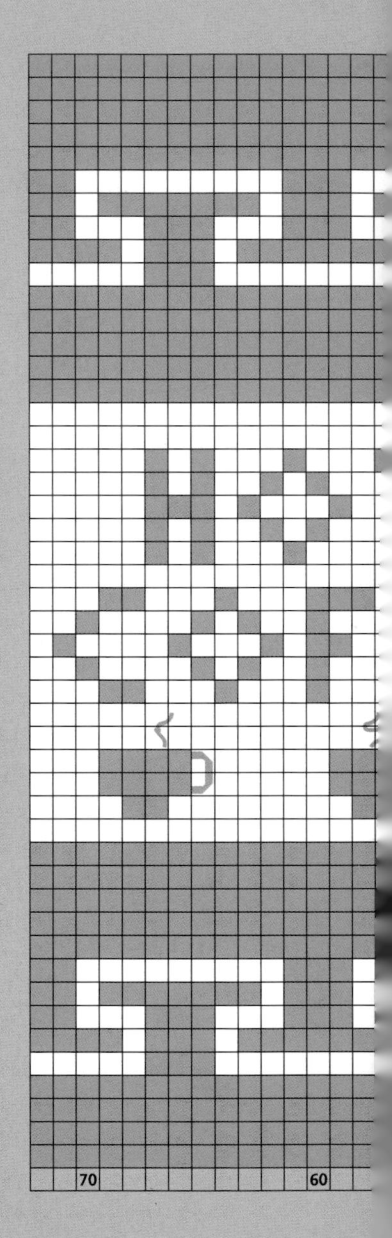

70
60

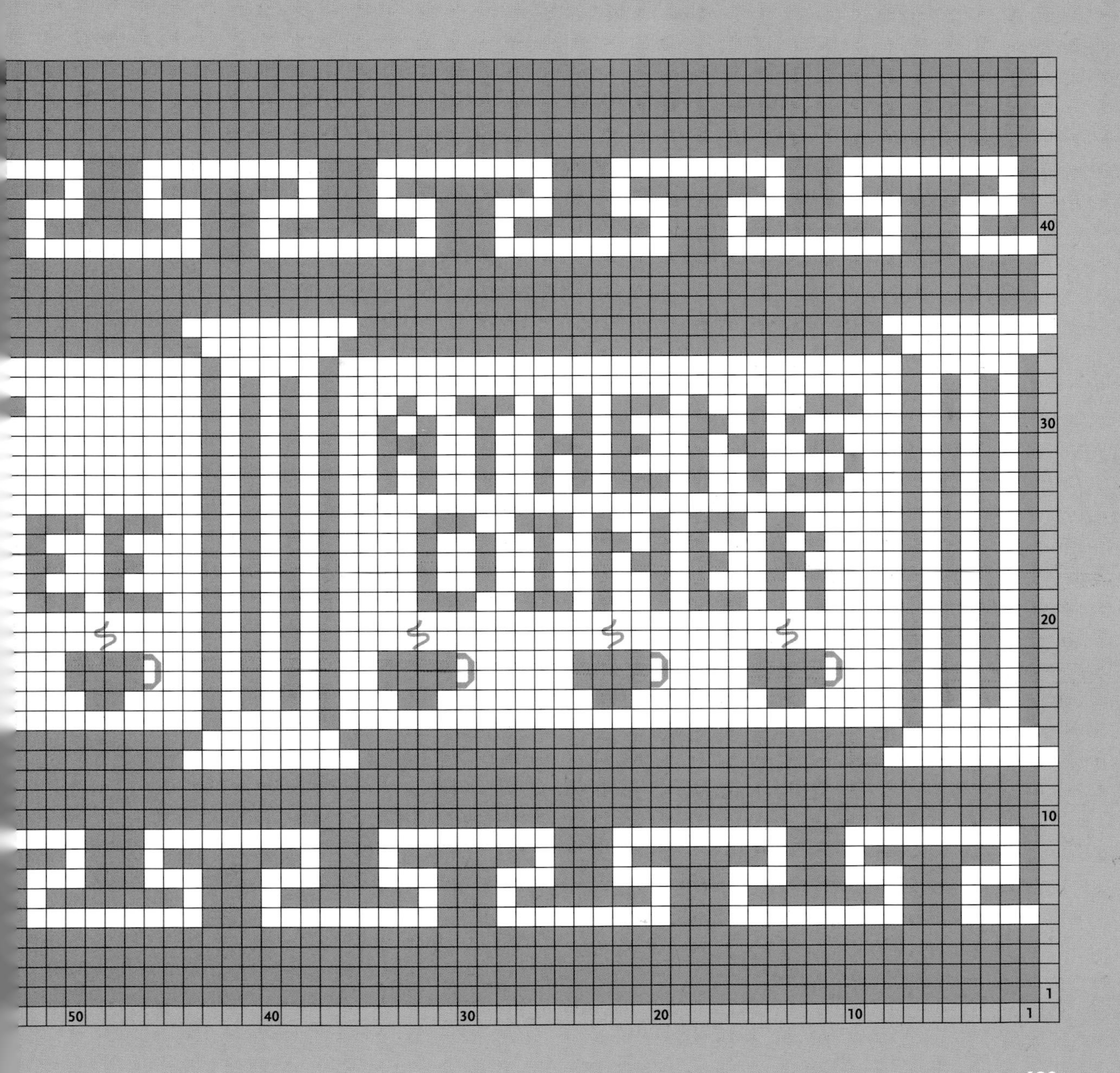
40
30
20
10
1
50
40
30
20
10
1

YARN INDEX

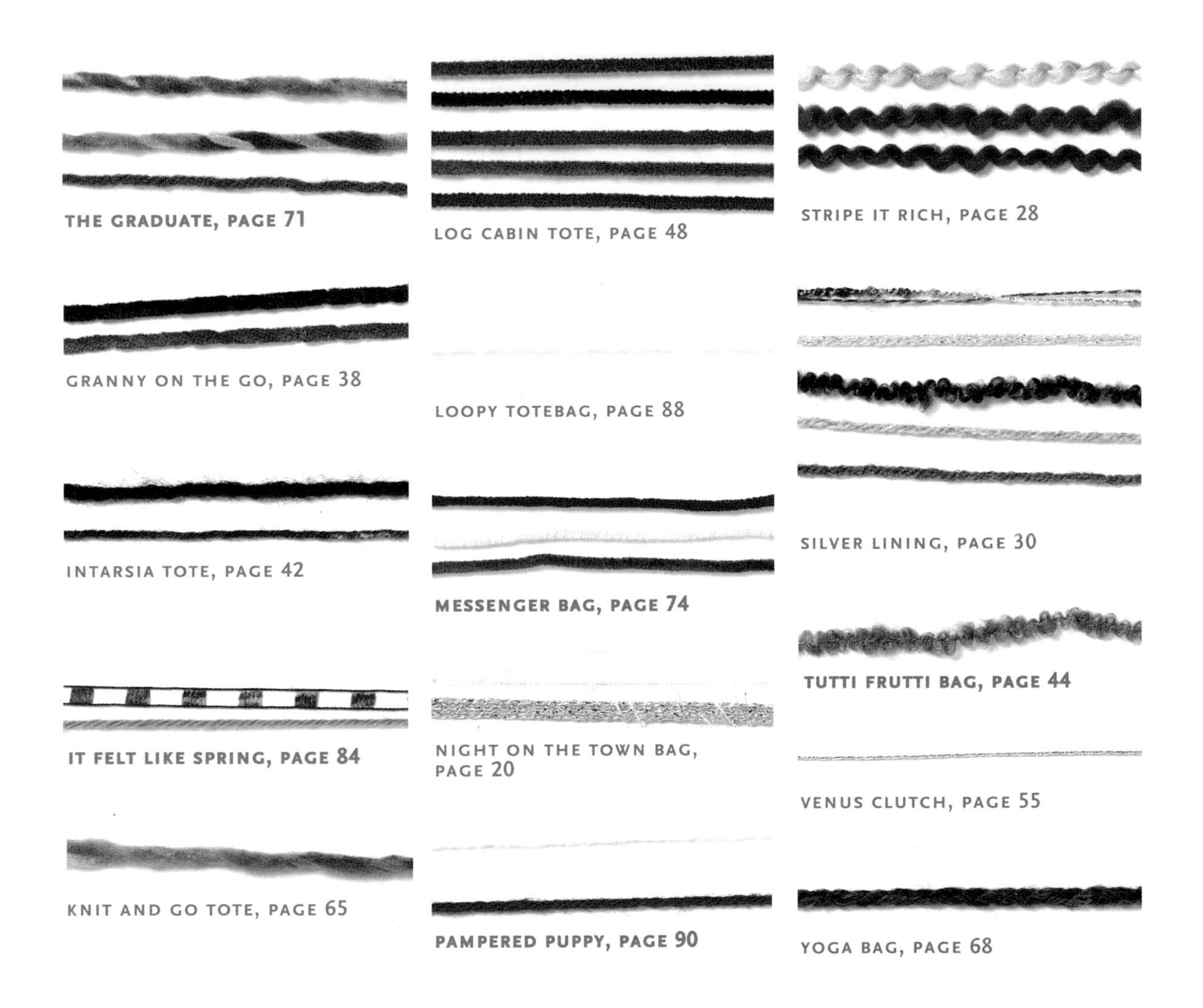
THE GRADUATE, PAGE 71
GRANNY ON THE GO, PAGE 38
INTARSIA TOTE, PAGE 42
IT FELT LIKE SPRING, PAGE 84
KNIT AND GO TOTE, PAGE 65
LOG CABIN TOTE, PAGE 48
LOOPY TOTEBAG, PAGE 88
MESSENGER BAG, PAGE 74
NIGHT ON THE TOWN BAG, PAGE 20
PAMPERED PUPPY, PAGE 90
STRIPE IT RICH, PAGE 28
SILVER LINING, PAGE 30
TUTTI FRUTTI BAG, PAGE 44
VENUS CLUTCH, PAGE 55
YOGA BAG, PAGE 68

INDEX